WHO'S RUNNING THIS KINGDOM?

PAM & STAN CAMPBELL

WHO'S RUNNING THIS KINGDOM?

VICTOR BOOKS

A DIVISION OF SCRIPTURE PRESS PUBLICATIONS INC.
USA CANADA ENGLAND

BibleLog Thru the Old Testament Series
Book 1   Let There Be Life (Genesis thru Ruth)
Book 2   Who's Running This Kingdom? (1 Samuel thru 2 Chronicles)
Book 3   Tales, Tunes, and Truths (Ezra thru Song of Songs)
Book 4   Watchmen Who Wouldn't Quit (Isaiah thru Malachi)

BibleLog Thru the New Testament Series
Book 1   When God Left Footprints (Matthew thru John)
Book 2   Good News to Go (Acts thru 1 Corinthians)
Book 3   Priority Mail (2 Corinthians thru Philemon)
Book 4   Home At Last (Hebrews thru Revelation)

BibleLog for Adults is an inductive Bible study series designed to take you through the Bible in 2 years if you study one session each week. This eight-book series correlates with SonPower's **BibleLog** Series for youth. You may want to use **BibleLog** in your daily quiet time, completing a chapter a week by working through a few pages each day. Or you may want to use this series (along with the SonPower **BibleLog** Series) in family devotions with your teenagers. This book also includes a leader's guide for use in small groups.

Scripture taken from the *Holy Bible, New International Version* ®. Copyright © 1973, 1978, 1984 by International Bible Society. Used by permission of Zondervan Publishing House. All rights reserved.

Designer: Joe DeLeon
Cover Illustration: Jeff Nishinaka
Interior Illustrations: Arnie Ten

Library of Congress Catalog Card Number: 92-82617
ISBN: 0-89693-872-7

Recommended Dewey Decimal Classification: 221
Suggested Subject Heading:BIBLE STUDY: OLD TESTAMENT

1 2 3 4 5 6 7 8 9 10 Print/Year 96   95   94   93   92

C O N T E N T S

BEFORE YOU BEGIN

Welcome to Book 2 in the
BibleLog Thru the Old Testament Series

Though the Bible continues to be one of the world's best-selling books, few people are familiar enough with it to comprehend "the big picture." They may know many of the specific stories about Abraham, Samson, Jonah, Jesus, Peter, Paul, and so forth. Yet most people are unsure how these characters fit into the broad historic groupings—patriarchs, judges, kings, prophets, Gospels, epistles, etc.

That's why we are introducing the **BibleLog Thru the Old Testament Series.** The purpose of the **BibleLog** studies is to guide you through the Old Testament in one year, at the rate of one session per week. This series eliminates the perceived drudgery of Bible reading by removing unnecessary references and explaining the material in clear terms that anyone can understand. The pace should be fast enough to propel you through the material without getting bogged down, yet slow enough to allow you to see things you never noticed before. First-time readers will feel completely at ease as they explore the Bible on their own. Yet no matter how many times the person has been through the Bible, this study will provide fresh insight.

WHAT MAKES BIBLELOG DIFFERENT?
Countless thousands of adults have, at some point in their lives, decided to read through the Bible. Pastors, Sunday School teachers, Bible study leaders, or peers have preached the benefits of "Read your Bible," "Get into the Word," "Meditate on Scripture," and so forth. And after hearing so many worthwhile challenges, a lot of determined, committed adults have dusted off the covers of their Bibles and set themselves to the task ahead.

They usually make a noble effort too. The first couple of Bible books whiz past before they know it. The next few books aren't quite as fast-paced, but they have their strong points. Then comes a tough passage. In most cases, the Gospels are enough to do in even the most eager readers. And instead of feeling like they've accomplished something, all those people feel is guilt because they didn't finish what they started.

6

That's why this Bible study series was developed. It calls for a one-year commitment on your part to get through the Old Testament. By following the session plans provided, you only need to complete one session each week to accomplish your one-year goal. You won't read the entire Old Testament word for word, but you will go much more in-depth than most of the Old Testament overviews you may have tried. You will still be challenged just to get through the major flow of Old Testament action in one year.

WHAT ARE THE FEATURES OF BIBLELOG?

- ❑ **THE WHOLE BIBLE** Not a verse-by-verse study, but an approach that hits all the books without skipping major passages.

- ❑ **THE RIGHT PACE** By completing one session each week (a couple of pages per day), you will get through the Old Testament in one year.

- ❑ **A FRESH APPROACH** The inductive design allows you to personally interact with biblical truth. Longer, drier passages are summarized in the text, and difficult passages are explained, but you are kept involved in the discovery process at all times.

- ❑ **INSTANT APPLICATION** Each weekly session concludes with a **Journey Inward** section of practical application that allows you to respond to the content immediately. The goal is to help you apply the truths of the Bible today.

- ❑ **GROUP STUDY OPTION** A leader's guide is included to promote discussion and further application if desired. After a week of self-study, a time of group interaction can be very effective in reinforcing God's truth. Each book covers 13 weeks.

- ❑ **REASONABLE PRICE** The entire set of 4 Old Testament **BibleLog** books costs no more than a basic Bible commentary. And after completing the series, you will have a self-written commentary of the Old Testament for future reference.

- ❑ **48 DIFFERENT TOPICS** Over a one-year period of study, you will be challenged to apply what the Bible has to say about 48 different topics, including God's sovereignty, murder, homosexuality, obedience, family relationships, and much more.

HOW CAN YOU GET THE MOST OUT OF BIBLELOG?

We recommend a group study for this series, if possible. If group members work through the content of the sessions individually during the week, the time your group needs to spend going over facts will be greatly reduced. With the content portion completed prior to the group meeting, your group time can emphasize the application of the biblical concepts to your individual members. A leader's guide is included at the back of the book to direct you in a review of the content. But the real strength of the leader's guide is to show you how to apply what you are learning. If you don't have the opportunity to go through this series with a group, that's OK too. Just be sure to think through all of the **Journey Inward** sections at the end of each session.

FROM THE AUTHORS

As you work through Book 2 in the **BibleLog Series,** expect to see a lot of contrasts. One you can't miss is God's love and perfection contrasted with mankind's sinfulness and disobedience.

Second, the Old Testament heroes and heroines, even with their many shortcomings, stand in bold contrast to the many wicked men you will read about. A third contrast to look for is in the results of choices. When a character chooses to do what God wants him or her to do, keep your eyes open for what happens to that character.

Contrast that person's life with a character who chooses not to do what God has instructed. Finally, look for comparisons and contrasts in your life and the lives of these Old Testament characters–both the good ones and the bad ones.

Here's a challenge to get you started, taken from the section of the Old Testament you are about to study.

> "Do not let this Book of the Law depart from your mouth; meditate on it day and night, so that you may be careful to do everything written in it. Then you will be prosperous and successful" (Joshua 1:8).

Pam & Stan Campbell

What is the stupidest dare you ever took?

1

YOU ASKED FOR IT!
(1 Samuel 1-10)

Occasionally, all of us do some incredibly dumb things just because someone dares us. Somehow, we disconnect our rational mental processes and imagine that nothing *too* bad will happen if we "uphold our honor" and accept the dare. As kids, some of us jumped off roofs. Or dived headfirst into a lake, not knowing how deep the water was. Or walked through a graveyard at midnight, trying our best not to panic. More recently, we may have drag raced down the freeway or tried schussing down the expert ski slope. Try to remember the stupidest dare you ever took. What did you do?

Do you remember how your parents responded when they discovered the ridiculous dares you took? "You reap what you sow." "Look before you leap." "You get what you pay for." They wanted you to learn that actions have consequences. And if they do an adequate job of training, the next time you are standing on an overpass with a police SWAT truck driving underneath and your best friend says, "I dare you to spit," you may think twice before you accept the dare.

Even though you've probably outgrown the need to take dares, you may not have mastered the art of avoiding actions that have delayed consequences. You don't hang up your clothes one day, you neglect to pick up the leftover dishes the next day, and before you know it, cleaning the house is a week-long project.

Or you go to a party, nibble all night on potato chips and mango dip, hot fudge sundaes, anchovy-onion-deluxe pizza, and burrito puffs. It all tastes great going down, but the next morning you realize you've made a terrible mistake. Your actions, and occasionally your *lack* of action, will have consequences at some point in the future.

You'll have a better opportunity to consider *your* actions and consequences in the **Journey Inward** section (at the end of this session), but first let's take a look at the actions and consequences of several biblical characters.

 JOURNEY ONWARD

If you completed the first book in the **BibleLog Thru the Old Testament Series**, *Let There Be Life,* you should remember that the Israelites have been delivered from their slavery in Egypt and have taken possession of Canaan— God's Promised Land. But they failed to run out all the inhabitants of the land, and quickly turned away from the standards God had set for them in order to do whatever *they* wanted to do. That is still the basic spiritual condition of the people as this book picks up at the beginning of 1 Samuel.

Read 1 Samuel 1:1-28.
The Book of 1 Samuel begins with the story of a person who is an exception to the do-your-own-thing attitude of most of the Israelites. The person's name is Hannah, and she had a problem. What was Hannah's problem? (1:1-8)

Getting Personal – *Have you (or anyone you know) suffered a problem similar to Hannah's? How are the childless couples you know dealing with their disappointment?*

12

Even though her husband did everything he could to encourage Hannah, her problem continued to trouble her. What made the problem even worse? (1:6)

What did Hannah decide to do about her problem? (1:9-11)

Eli, the priest, saw Hannah and didn't understand what she was doing. What advice did he give her? (1:12-14)

When Hannah explained what she was doing, what did Eli tell her then? (1:15-17)

Read 1 Samuel 2:1-26.
Hannah was encouraged after her trip to the temple and her talk with Eli. She had good cause to be—later she gave birth to a son and named him Samuel. And true to her word, she dedicated him to God. As soon as Samuel was old enough to leave home, Hannah took him to the temple to grow up under the authority of Eli, the priest. Hannah didn't seem to mourn her decision. Rather, she rejoiced in God's power that could give her a son in the first place, and she praised God in a wonderful prayer (2:1-10).

Samuel wasn't the only person under Eli's care. Eli had two sons of his own—Hophni and Phinehas. What kind of people were Eli's sons? (2:12-17)

Getting Personal — *Do you know anyone whose children seem to have something in common with Eli's sons? How can you encourage and support the parents?*

Eli was glad to have Samuel around, and he probably realized what a sacrifice it had been for Hannah to give up her only child. When she made her annual sacrifice at the temple and took Samuel a new set of clothes, Eli would pray for her to have more children. What was the result of these prayers? (2:18-21)

As time passed, the contrast between Samuel and the sons of Eli became greater and greater. Eli knew how wicked his sons were. (By this time they were sleeping with the women who worked at God's temple.) He scolded them, but he apparently never disciplined them. He told them that there was no one to intercede for someone who sins willingly against God, but they wouldn't listen. Yet while Hophni and Phinehas got worse, Samuel grew to be a person pleasing to both God and other people. Finally God sent a messenger to Eli with a prophecy.

Read 1 Samuel 2:27-36.
What was prophesied for Eli's family line?

What was prophesied for Eli's sons?

What was prophesied for the future of the priesthood?

Read 1 Samuel 3:1-21.
Explain how Samuel learned to communicate with God.

Getting Personal – *How do you communicate with God?*

God's first message to Samuel was a lot for a young boy to handle. After all, just the night before, Samuel had Eli to thank for being able to hear what God had to say. But God's message was that He was about to bring judgment on Eli's family because of the wickedness of Eli's sons. And Eli was also to be punished because he hadn't done anything to stop his sons after he learned of their grievous sins.

Samuel didn't want to have to confront Eli with that bit of news. But Eli encouraged Samuel to be truthful with him. Samuel then told him everything, and Eli accepted it—not as Samuel's message, but as the word of the Lord. Soon all the people of Israel had come to realize that Samuel was indeed a powerful prophet of God.

Fighting the Philistines

The people certainly needed a valid prophet of God during this time. They were quickly discovering that God was not automatically going to heap blessings upon them just because they called themselves God's people, yet didn't act like it. For instance, they went to battle against the Philistines. The Israelites were defeated and 4,000 of them died. The elders of Israel couldn't understand why God had allowed them to be defeated, and they came to the conclusion that perhaps all they needed to do was to carry the ark of the covenant in front of the army. (While it is true that God's presence was associated with the ark of the covenant, the people were equating the ark to a divine good-luck symbol. To them, sending for the ark was about equivalent to sending for a rabbit's foot or a supply of four-leaf clovers.)

Read 1 Samuel 4:1-22.
The presence of the ark in the Israelite camp caused a great excitement. The people of Israel raised such a great shout that the ground shook. The Philistines were a little shaken when they discovered that the Israelites had brought in the ark, but what other effect did it have on them? (4:4-9)

What were the major results of the battle that followed? (4:10-11)

The news of the battle had a great impact on many of the people who heard it. One person who was severely affected was Eli. How did he respond when the messenger brought him the battle results? (4:12-18)

Another person affected by the news was the wife of Phinehas, who was in the last months of a pregnancy. She heard the news about the ark and the deaths of Eli and Phinehas all at once, went into labor, and died shortly after giving birth. But before she died, she gave her new son the symbolic name of Ichabod, which means "no glory." Why did she choose this name? (4:19-22)

Read 1 Samuel 5:1-12.
After the battle, the Philistines had the Israelite ark of the covenant, but they didn't quite know what to do with it. The first thing they did was take it to their temple and set it up beside their god, Dagon. What was the first hint they received that this might have been a mistake? (5:1-4)

What was the second hint they received? (5:6-7)

When no one was willing to let the Israelite ark of the covenant be placed in their city, what did the Philistines decide to do with it? (5:11-12)

Read 1 Samuel 6:1-21.
The ark had been in Philistine territory for seven months, and the Philistines didn't want to keep it any longer than they had to. But they didn't want to further upset Israel's God, so they wanted to be careful how they went about

returning the ark. The Philistine priests were consulted, and they determined that the ark should not be returned unless an offering was included. What offering did they decide to send back with the ark, and why was that particular offering selected? (6:4-5)

But the Philistines still weren't 100 percent sure that the God of Israel was causing their sufferings. What test did they use to determine whether or not it was necessary for them to return the ark? (6:7-9)

Their test had the expected results and the ark was returned to Israel. How was it received when it arrived there? (6:13-16)

Some of the Israelite men didn't show proper respect for the ark when it was returned to Israel. What did they do that was wrong, and what happened to them? (6:19-20)

Read 1 Samuel 7:1–8:3.
The ark was then taken to a place where it could stay for a while—the house of a man named Abinadab. (He and his family took care of the ark for the next 100 years.) The 20 years after the return of the ark was a period of spiritual renewal for the Israelites. Samuel was active in convincing them to put aside all their idol gods and worship the true God alone. They obeyed his instructions and then met together for a time of fasting and confession.

When the Philistines heard that the Israelites had assembled, they gathered together their own army and prepared for battle. The Israelites were frightened and asked Samuel to pray for them. Samuel offered a lamb to the

Lord, and God protected the Israelites. How did Israel win the battle that day? (7:10-13)

As long as Samuel led the Israelites, the Philistines did no real damage. But as Samuel got older, he appointed his sons to judge Israel. How did that system work? (8:1-3)

Plan B: A King
Read 1 Samuel 8:4-22.
The Israelites decided it was time for them to have a king. Why did they want one? (8:4-5)

Samuel was disappointed when the people approached him with their request. But he responded the way he did to almost any crisis—he prayed. What did God tell him was the reason the people wanted a king? (8:7)

God wanted Samuel to explain to the people exactly what having a king would mean to them. What were some of the things Samuel brought up? (8:10-18)

How well did Samuel change the minds of the Israelites? (8:19-22)

Read 1 Samuel 9:1-27.
It seems that since the people demanded a king, God decided to provide one

that they could easily see. What was the name of the man, and what was distinctive about him? (9:1-2, 17)

When Samuel first saw the man who was to be Israel's new king, the guy was on the "royal" assignment of looking for his father's lost donkeys. And he wasn't even doing a good job of that. (He couldn't find them.) But Saul and his servant had heard that Samuel was somewhere in the area. They figured if they could find Samuel, he could direct them to the lost donkeys. Of course, God had told Samuel to expect Saul. When Saul showed up, Samuel was supposed to anoint him king over Israel. How did Saul respond when he heard the news? (9:19-21)

Getting Personal — *Put yourself in Saul's place. How would you have responded to Samuel's news?*

Read 1 Samuel 10:1-27.
Samuel had Saul over for dinner, they talked, and Samuel anointed him, signifying that God had chosen Saul as king. Then Samuel gave Saul some instructions and some signs to look for to prove that God was with him. Everything occurred just as Samuel predicted. (One of the specific instructions Samuel gave Saul was to meet him at a place called Gilgal in seven days. This instruction will be referred to in the next session.)

As Saul left Samuel, "God changed Saul's heart" (10:9). When Saul got home, he told his family that Samuel had helped him find the donkeys, but he didn't tell them anything else at first. And when Samuel called together all the Israelites to anoint their new king publicly, Saul could not be found. Where was he? (10:17-24)

The next session will examine the details of the life of Israel's first, and apparently publicity-shy, king.

 JOURNEY INWARD

As mentioned earlier in this session, it is important to give some serious thought to **actions and their consequences**. The biblical content of this session is filled with examples—both positive and negative. For example:

❏ Hannah's action (prayer) resulted in the ability to finally have a child (several children, in fact).
❏ Eli's lack of action toward his sons resulted in the deaths of his entire family.
❏ Israel's willing disobedience to God resulted in their defeat at the hands of the Philistines.
❏ The Philistines' irreverent treatment of the ark of God resulted in plagues throughout their land.
❏ And the Israelites' demand for a king, though the people didn't really know it yet, would result in all the consequences that Samuel predicted.

Notice the direct relationship between actions and consequences. A positive, good action usually has good results, and negative actions usually have negative results. Think of your own life during the past few weeks. What is one action you took that had good results?

What is one action you took that had bad results?

What is one action you took where you won't know the results for a while?

20

Think of a couple of people you know who took an action on something a long time ago and are still experiencing the consequences of that action. Describe the circumstances below.

Do you think it is possible for God to forgive a sin, but still allow you to live with the consequences of that sin? Explain your answer.

Many of your decisions could have significant results. The amount of time you decide to spend studying could determine which graduate school you can (or can't) attend. The person you decide to date and eventually marry *could* be HIV positive. The full-time job you choose can influence your career choices.

All these choices could be very scary if you were the only person involved in making them. But you're not. God wants to be included in helping determine what actions you take so the consequences of those actions will be what is best for you. The story of Samuel as a boy in the temple is a good example, demonstrating that even young children can develop their "spiritual" side. God does speak to us through youth leaders, pastors, Sunday School teachers, and friends. But this example also points out that it might be easy to confuse God's instructions with other people's instructions (especially if it's a new practice for you). Make a list of actions you can take this week that will result in the positive consequences of more effective communication with God.

Samuel is also noteworthy for obeying God, even though it was a difficult assignment. What is the hardest thing you think God could ask you to do?

If God *did* decide to ask you to do what you just listed, would you do it or not? Why? And what do you think would be the consequences of your decision?

Another lesson to be learned about actions and consequences comes at the expense of the Philistines. They did something they shouldn't have (stole the ark of the covenant) and they suffered for it. Are you currently involved in something you shouldn't be (cheating, lying, drinking, gossip, sexual activity, etc.)? And if so, do you suffer for it in any way?

Finally, can you think of anything you really desire that you think may not be God's will for you (like the Israelites' desire for a king)? When you think of an example, make a list of all the possible harm that could come from your decision.

Whether or not you continue will still be your decision. But just as Samuel listed all the negative effects of having a king, you need to make yourself aware of all the possible side-effects of *your* desire. Then if you decide to continue it and suffer the consequences, you can only blame yourself—not God.

KEY VERSE

"Speak, Lord, for Your servant is listening" (1 Samuel 3:9).

Our society seems to honor size.

2

THE BIGGER THEY ARE . . .

(1 Samuel 11–17)

Our society seems to honor size. Most men would love to add another inch or so to their height. Football players and weight lifters don't just want to *be* good; they want to *look* good. And how many single women do you know who daydream of finding a guy who is *short*, dark, and handsome? Yet in this session, you should discover that a lot of height doesn't necessarily insure a lot of peace of mind, wisdom, or courage.

 JOURNEY ONWARD

Read 1 Samuel 11:1-15.

In the last session you saw the call of Israel's first king—Saul, the son of Kish, who stood a head taller than anyone else. No sooner was Saul anointed than he was faced with several challenges. One problem was within his own ranks—a group of people started murmuring against Saul, saying, "How can this fellow save us?" (1 Samuel 10:27) Saul decided to let this problem go, and did nothing to silence the troublemakers.

The second problem was more severe. The Ammonites had threatened some of the Israelites (in the city of Jabesh Gilead). The Israelites there had agreed to make a treaty with the Ammonites and become their servants, but the Ammonites weren't quite satisfied. What did they expect the Israelites to do in addition? (11:1-2)

Naturally the Israelites were reluctant to comply with the Ammonites' request, so they turned to their new king for help. Saul knew he needed to put together an army in a hurry. How did he do it? (11:6-7)

How many men did Saul recruit? (11:8)

The Israelites who had been approached by the Ammonites faked a surrender, giving Saul's men enough time to surround the Ammonite camp and thoroughly defeat the Ammonites. After proving himself a capable king, Saul had a lot of support from the Israelites. In fact, the people wanted to find the troublemakers who had been murmuring against Saul and have them put to death. But Saul refused to allow it. Why? (11:12-13)

Read 1 Samuel 12:1-25.
And with Saul established as leader of the Israelites, Samuel at this time decided to give his farewell address to the people of Israel. He began by asking if anyone could charge him with any wrongdoing, which, of course, no one could. By publicly affirming that he had not used his position for his personal benefit, Samuel sets a positive example for the people who are to follow him. Then Samuel gave a mini-review of the history of Israel to remind the people of the Lord's faithfulness to them. What were some of the events he recalled? (12:8-11)

Getting Personal – *What events can you recall of God's faithfulness?*

Samuel followed his review with a warning concerning the people's request for a king. What warning did he give the Israelites? (12:13-15)

After his warning, Samuel gave the people a sign to show that their request for a human king was an indication of their rejection of God as their king, and was not what God wanted for them. What was the sign? (12:16-18)

The Israelites were frightened when they realized that they had rejected God, and they asked Samuel to pray for them. Samuel explained that if they would serve God in the future, God would not reject them. It wasn't that God couldn't lead the Israelites with a king; it was that a human king could never successfully lead the people without God's leadership. And what did Samuel promise the Israelites he would do? (12:23)

Read 1 Samuel 13:1-22.
Saul's next challenge was the Philistine army. Saul's oldest son, Jonathan, attacked a Philistine outpost, and the Philistine army began to gather to fight against Israel. How big was the Philistine army? (13:5)

How did Israel react to the gathering of the Philistines? (13:6-7)

While the two armies were gathering for battle, the time came when Saul was supposed to meet Samuel at Gilgal. (This meeting was the one they scheduled at the end of the last session. See 1 Samuel 10:8.) The seventh day had come, but Samuel was not there yet. Saul looked around at his frightened army, and saw that many of the men were beginning to sneak away. He figured that before long he wouldn't have much of an army at all to go against the Philistines, so he decided to take the matter into his own hands. Even though Samuel had instructed Saul to wait until he (Samuel) could present a burnt offering to God, Saul tried to restore Israel's morale and insure God's favor in battle by going ahead with the offering in Samuel's absence. As soon as Saul had made the offering, Samuel showed up. Saul tried to make excuses for his actions, but what did Samuel tell him? (13:13-14)

Having been rebuked by Samuel, Saul turned his attention to the Philistines who were in the area. What major disadvantage did the Israelites face as they prepared for war against the Philistines? (13:19-22)

Read 1 Samuel 14:1-52.
Saul's son, Jonathan, decided to lead a raid on the Philistines by himself
(with the help of his armor-bearer). Why wasn't he afraid of being outnumbered? (14:6)

Jonathan and his armor-bearer decided on a sign as to whether or not to go
forward after the Philistines had spotted them. What was to determine
whether or not they should attack the Philistines? (14:8-10)

After receiving the sign indicating they should go ahead, Jonathan and his
armor-bearer entered the Philistine camp. The two of them killed 20
Philistines right away, and God supported their efforts. How? (14:15)

The Israelite army noticed the disorganization in the Philistine ranks, and
Saul immediately began to look around to see who was missing. After he
discovered that Jonathan and his armor-bearer were gone, he hurried his
men into battle. When the Israelites arrived at the battle scene, they
discovered that the Philistines were so confused that they were killing each
other with their swords. As the Israelites began to pursue the fleeing
Philistines, they gathered support from many people who had been living
with the Philistines and others who had been hiding in the hill country.

As the Israelites began to chase down the Philistines, Saul put the people
under a strict oath. What did he forbid the people to do, and how long was
the prohibition to be in effect? (14:24)

Who broke the oath, and why did he break it? (14:25-30)

By the end of the day, the Israelites who had followed Saul's instructions
were exhausted and famished. And because of their physical condition, they
committed a sin which they knew they shouldn't do. What was their sin?
(14:31-35)

After Saul made an offering on behalf of the sinful Israelites, he wanted to continue his pursuit of the Philistines throughout the night. The people were in agreement, but a priest who was there suggested that they check to see what God had to say about the idea. But when Saul asked God what to do, he couldn't get an answer. Saul realized that some sin must have occurred to prevent God from answering and giving the Israelites clear directions. He boldly swore to discover and take care of the sin, even if it meant the death of his son, Jonathan.

Saul didn't know how close to the truth he was. After casting lots, Saul discovered that Jonathan *was* at fault for eating food in defiance of Saul's oath. (True, Jonathan didn't disobey on purpose because he didn't even know about Saul's oath. If anything, Saul was probably at fault for telling his army to take an oath before making sure that they were all there. But an oath was not to be taken lightly. Even though it had been broken unintentionally, God could not bless His people until the broken oath was dealt with.) And when Saul found out that Jonathan was the guilty party, he decreed that Jonathan must die. What happened that changed Saul's mind? (14:44-45)

Even though Jonathan was allowed to live, the Israelites didn't get to continue following the Philistines. As a result, the Philistines escaped to their own land. But nevertheless, Saul was making a name as a heroic leader. He led Israel to victories against the Moabites, Edomites, Ammonites, Amalekites, and other enemies.

Obey, OK?
Read 1 Samuel 15:1-35.
Saul might have continued to be victorious, but he had a real problem doing what he was told. Just as he had previously ignored Samuel's instructions at Gilgal, he again disobeyed God's instructions. God was going to bring judgment on the Amalekites at the hands of Saul and the Israelites. What did God tell Saul to do? (15:1-3)

Notice how clear the instructions were. But what did Saul do instead? (15:7-9)

29

In the last session you examined the relationships between actions and their consequences. In this instance, Saul's actions had an effect on both God and Samuel. How did God feel that Saul had disobeyed Him? (15:10-11)

What was the effect on Samuel?

In the meantime, Saul was out building monuments to himself (15:12). And when Samuel approached him, Saul proudly declared that he had done what God had asked him to do. Samuel's response was rather sarcastic. What did Samuel say to Saul? (15:14)

Getting Personal – *What kinds of monuments to yourself have you built? What have been the results?*

Samuel tried to explain that Saul had been entrusted with an important mission from God, and that he had disregarded God's specific instructions. But Saul continued to try to defend himself. He stuck to his story that he had done what God had asked of him. Saul had convinced himself that it was OK to ignore what God had said as long as he made an offering to God in return. What did Samuel tell Saul about his mistaken thinking? (15:22-23)

What do you think Samuel meant when he told Saul, "To obey is better than sacrifice"?

Getting Personal –*Are there times when you would rather sacrifice than obey? If so, when?*

Saul hadn't seemed too concerned about the consequences of his actions on anyone else, but the fact that God was planning to remove him as king gradually began to sink in. He confessed his sin, asked Samuel to go with him, and apparently hoped everything would be OK again. But Samuel reemphasized that God had rejected Saul as king. Samuel turned to go, and Saul tried to stop him by grabbing his robe. The robe tore, and Samuel used the incident as an illustration. What did he tell Saul the torn robe represented? (15:27-29)

Samuel finally went with Saul and worshiped with him. But while he was there, Samuel attended to the business that Saul had neglected. What did Samuel do? (15:32-33)

Read 1 Samuel 16:1-23.
This was Samuel's last visit with Saul. Even though Samuel had foretold the problems that would come to Israel along with their insistence of a king, it appears that Samuel was optimistic that Saul, at least, would work out for a while. But God made it clear to Samuel that Saul had been rejected. With this in mind, God told Samuel to go anoint the person God had chosen to replace Saul. Notice Samuel's reaction. What was he worried about? (16:1-2)

God led Samuel to the home of a man named Jesse, who had several sons. The first son presented to Samuel was the eldest, named Eliab. What was Samuel's response to Eliab? (16:6)

What did God tell Samuel regarding Eliab? (16:7)

What happened then? (16:8-13)

From the day that Samuel anointed Jesse's son, David, the Spirit of God was with David. And at the same time, King Saul began to suffer from the presence of an evil spirit. Saul's advisers told him he should hire a musician to play for him, and through God's planning Saul hired David, a trained harp player. Saul liked David. When Saul felt the evil spirit, David would play the harp and the evil spirit would leave.

Now at this time people knew very little about David, but what did they think about him? (16:18)

Giant-Sized Problem
Read 1 Samuel 17:1-58.
Israel was still at war with the Philistines. In fact, the Israelites were just beginning to realize what kind of trouble they were in. What was the main problem faced by the Israelites as they opposed the Philistines? (17:3-10)

How were they responding to their problem? Why? (17:11)

How long had they had this particular problem? (17:16)

During this time, David was commuting back and forth from his father's home to Saul's court. On this specific occasion, David was just returning from home with some food Jesse had sent for David's brothers in Saul's army. And just as David arrived, he saw (and heard) Goliath come out for his daily challenge to play one-on-one with any single Israelite. David learned from some of the Israelite soldiers that King Saul had offered big rewards for any person who was able to defeat Goliath: Saul's daughter as his wife, great wealth, and a permanent tax exemption. What was David's reaction to this information? (17:26)

How did David's brother react? (17:28)

David volunteered to fight Goliath, but Saul was reluctant to allow him to do so. What was Saul's objection and David's response to that objection? (17:33-37)

Even after Saul agreed to let David go fight Goliath, Saul tried to help him out. How? (17:38-39)

Why didn't David agree to Saul's offer of help?

How did David prepare for his fight? (17:40)

What was Goliath's reaction to David? (17:41-44)

Was David confident as he approached Goliath? Why? (17:45-47)

No doubt you know how the fight turned out. But review 1 Samuel 17:48-54 and write down any new information that you didn't already know.

The next session will cover some of the repercussions of the battle between David and Goliath, but for now David is a hero in everyone's eyes. He is a colorful example of what God can do through someone who has faith enough to put his total confidence in Him. But sometimes we don't think God can use "little old me." And that's what the rest of this session is about.

JOURNEY INWARD

Several incidents in this session can teach us some valuable lessons about **judging people based on outer appearances.** Remember how Beauty mustered enough mercy to kiss the Beast so he too could become a handsome creature. Or how the beautiful princess appeared dead, but in reality she was only sleeping. The secret that brings out the truth in each case is love.

Of course, the principle works both ways. Any good fairy tale connoisseur knows he should watch out for wolves in sheep's clothing (or dressed as Red Riding Hood's grandmother), for witch houses disguised as gingerbread castles or, as Snow White learned, for witches in the guise of little-old-lady apple sellers.

But as much as fairy tales and Bible stories encourage us not to judge people by outer appearances, we usually end up doing it anyway. As you have seen, even many of the major characters of the Bible were deceived by looks. Take Samuel, for instance. As he examined Eliab, David's oldest brother, Samuel was sure this must be the person God intended to be the next king of Israel. But God had to remind Samuel not to judge according to height or other outer appearances. In the space below, list people you tend to judge primarily on physical appearance. Include examples of those you rate highly (possibly athletes, music performers, actors, coworkers, etc.) as well as those you tend to look down on (geeks, burnouts, street people, or whatever classifications the outcasts fall into these days).

PAW (Physical Appearance Winners)	PAL (Physical Appearance Losers)

Now take a look at your list of "winners." What negative characteristics might they have that could make them seem less attractive if you knew them better? What positive characteristics might your "losers" have if you knew them better?

How much does your opinion of these two separate columns affect the reality of their actual worthiness?

King Saul was another person guilty of judging on the basis of appearance. Goliath had all (but one) of the Israelites shaking in their boots. And when you think about it, King Saul was probably shaking more than the rest of them. If the Israelites decided to send out *their* tallest warrior to fight Goliath, Saul would have been the one to go (1 Samuel 9:2).

List below the people or problems that seem like Goliaths to you—those things you don't think you'll ever be able to conquer on your own.

Now choose five "stones" below that you would choose to combat the Goliath problems in your life.

Patience	Love	Inner Peace	Different Priorities
Courage	Hope	Tact	A Different Perspective
God's Help	Confidence	Sympathy	Energy
Power	More Time	Starting Over	Determination
Self-control	Hard Work	Forgiveness	Help from Friends

Finally, remember that David didn't claim to have killed Goliath on his own. He gave God all the credit for his victory. You probably won't be able to conquer your problems and people on your own either. Ask God to give you the strength to trust Him as you prepare to confront your "unbeatable" problems in the future.

 **KEY VERSE**
"To obey is better than sacrifice" (1 Samuel 15:22).

Few things hurt as much as false accusations.

3

JUST ONE KING
AFTER ANOTHER
(1 Samuel 18–23)

The story is told of a man who lived during the Revolutionary War. Though he lived in the colonies, he repeatedly spoke out in defense of the British. As the war intensified, the man became more vocal about how the colonial rebels were wrong and should submit to England. Not only did this man suffer a lot of verbal abuse and indignity, but his wife and children were persecuted as well. Threats of tar-and-feathering became common, yet this man continued to speak up for England—the biggest enemy of his new country.

When the Revolutionary War was over, George Washington himself visited the town where this man lived. Washington had something to say to this man, and he called a meeting of the townspeople so they could all hear what Washington would tell him. When everyone was assembled and Washington began to speak, the townspeople couldn't believe their ears. George Washington was actually *praising* this guy. But as the people listened, Washington explained to them that the man had been one of his spies throughout the entire war. Washington had hand picked him to form alliances with the British and discover whatever he could, and now Washington wanted to personally and publicly thank him for not giving in under pressure.

Put yourself in the man's place or as a member of his family. Can you imagine what an outcast you would have been at work or when you went to town? It's not likely that the man entrusted his secret to his family. But if you *had* known that your spouse wasn't really a traitor and was, in fact, a CIA agent for George Washington, could you have kept the secret when everyone started to pick on you?

Few things hurt as much as a false accusation and the persecution that comes from it. To be accused unjustly can cause great inner turmoil and an unquenchable desire to expose the truth. You know the feeling if you've ever:

- ❑ Been falsely accused of cheating
- ❑ Been stopped by a policeman for something you didn't do
- ❑ Had a parent blame you for something your brother or sister did
- ❑ Lost a good friend because someone spread a false rumor about you
- ❑ Had someone misunderstand you and start telling lies behind your back

 JOURNEY ONWARD

Read 1 Samuel 18:1-30.

Many times, the cause of false accusations and persecution is jealousy. Such was the case with David. The last session concluded with David's victory over Goliath, an event which made David an instant celebrity in Israel. After the giant had fallen and the Philistines were on the run, everyone wanted to know who their new, young hero was. Saul, for one, discovered that David's success was no fluke. He called David to work for him full-time and gave him new responsibilities, and David handled all of them well.

In the meantime, David found a new best friend—Saul's son, Jonathan. They made a covenant of friendship and promised to support each other, no matter what. Jonathan even gave his own robe, tunic, sword, bow, and belt to David.

Getting Personal — *Have you ever had a best friend? How was your relationship similar to David and Jonathan's friendship?*

But David's problems started when his celebrity status reached the public. He even had a song written about him. What were some of the lyrics? (18:6-7)

How did Saul respond when he heard the song, and why? (18:8-9)

Not surprisingly, Saul was plagued by his evil spirit again. But this time when David was called, his harp playing didn't seem to help Saul. What happened? (18:10-11)

Getting Personal – *Have you ever been in David's position of being envied by others? How did others respond to you?*

Saul realized that David had the power of God that Saul himself had once had, and he was afraid of David. It seemed a wise move to get David away for a while, so Saul made David commander over 1,000 men and sent him off to fight battles. Saul secretly hoped that David would be killed, but what happened instead? (18:12-16)

Another issue between David and Saul was Saul's promise of one of his daughters to marry whoever killed Goliath. Saul offered his older daughter, Merab, to David, but David was a little reluctant to marry into royalty. He seemed to think that a shepherd from a simple family had no right to become the king's son-in-law. Saul, of course, could have convinced David otherwise. After all, Saul had already promised his daughter to *anyone* who killed Goliath. And if you remember, when Saul was called to be king, he was out tending to lost donkeys. But instead of reasoning with David, Saul gave Merab to someone else to marry.

It just so happened that Saul's younger daughter, Michal, loved David. Saul heard of it and figured it would be a convenient way to fulfill his original promise to David. But David gave him the same excuse once again (18:23). It was normal in Israelite society at this time for the father of a bride to expect a gift from the prospective groom, and perhaps David didn't feel he had anything to offer a king. Saul asked for quite an unusual gift in exchange for Michal, but it was one that David was able to meet. What was it, and why did Saul ask for such a bizarre bride price? (18:24-25)

How did David respond to Saul's challenge? (18:26-27)

After David passed his test with flying colors, Saul was even more depressed about him. Saul knew a lot of people were beginning to give their love and loyalty to David—the Israelites, Jonathan, Michal—and now even God was helping David. And the harder Saul tried to set him up, the more successful David became.

Read 1 Samuel 19:1-24.
Jonathan knew of his father's attempts to kill David, and did all he could to protect his friend. He hid David for a while and went to reason with Saul about David's positive influence on Israel. Saul listened to Jonathan and took an oath not to harm David, but his new attitude didn't last long. David went back for a while to his usual responsibilities in Saul's court, but then war broke out again with the Philistines. Because of David's leadership, the Philistines were quickly driven back, and Saul again was so jealous that he tried to pin David to the wall with his spear. David dodged the spear and escaped.

Saul even had David's house staked out with the intention of having him killed in the morning. But Michal realized what was going on and came up with an elaborate plan to help David escape. What did she do? (19:11-17)

David still had an ally outside of Saul's home—Samuel, who at this time was training a group of prophets. David went to Samuel and told him everything that had been happening. As soon as Saul heard where he was, he sent men to capture David and bring him back. But as soon as Saul's men got there, God's spirit fell on them and they began to prophesy like the other prophets. Saul then sent another group of men, and another. Yet every time Saul's men got close to where David and Samuel were, they began to prophesy and were powerless to capture David. Finally Saul determined to go himself. What happened when he got to Samuel? (19:23-24)

Once David discovered that Saul knew where he was, it was no longer safe for him to stay with Samuel. David checked in with Jonathan to see what he could find out, but Jonathan knew nothing of his father's actions toward David. However, Jonathan agreed to do a little spying for David, and the two friends worked out a signal. David would hide in a nearby field while Jonathan made an excuse for David's absence and tested Saul's attitude. Jonathan would then return to the field with a boy servant and would shoot three arrows. If Saul was angry at David, Jonathan would tell the boy the arrows were beyond the target (a stone near the place David was hiding). If it were safe for David to return, Jonathan was to tell the boy that the arrows were short of their target. And before Jonathan left David, the two of them renewed their covenant of friendship.

Read 1 Samuel 20:1-42.
What happened when Jonathan went to see how Saul felt about David? (20:24-33)

Even though Jonathan had gone to all the trouble of working out a signal, it seems he couldn't leave without seeing David one more time. He sent the boy back to town, and he and David had a tearful good-bye. Then David left to continue his life as a fugitive.

Getting Personal – *How do you say good-bye to your good friends?*

Read 1 Samuel 21:1-15.
David went to a town called Nob where a group of priests lived. (By the time he got there, he had picked up a few followers.) Apparently, he wanted to meet with the priests to determine God's will for his life at that time. He asked the priests for food, but they had nothing except the bread that was offered to God daily and then removed. (This was the bread of the Presence that was placed on a special table in the tabernacle.) This bread was supposed to be eaten only by the priests, but the priest at Nob was willing to

make an exception as long as David and his followers were clean according to the Law (hadn't had sex lately, touched a dead body, etc.). David also made another request of the priests. What was his request and how did the priests answer it? (21:8-9)

David and his men weren't alone in the presence of the priests. Who else was there? (21:7)

After stocking up on food and borrowing a weapon, David left the priests of Nob and went to a city called Gath. This seems to be an unusual move, because Gath was one of five major cities of the Philistines, but perhaps David thought he might be able to remain anonymous. Did he? (21:10-11)

When David discovered that the Philistines recognized who he was, how did he respond? (21:12)

What did David do to avoid a serious conflict between himself and Achish, the king of Gath? (21:13-15)

Read 1 Samuel 22:1-23.
Even though Achish didn't seem eager to harm David, it appears that David thought it best to leave. Word of his new location (the cave of Adullam) reached his family, so his brothers and other relatives went to see him. Who else went there? (22:1-2)

David may have figured that since a rather large group of people knew where he was, Saul might get word as well. Anyway, David had a little more business to attend to — in Moab. What? (22:3-4)

You may remember in the story of Ruth that Ruth was David's great-grandmother, and she was from Moab. This gave David some weight as he tried to make a deal with the king of Moab. Besides, King Saul had previously fought against Moab (14:47), so in one sense David and the king of Moab were allies. But warned by a prophet not to stay in Moab, David and his men returned to Judah and hid in a forest.

Meanwhile, Saul *had* received word of David's recent whereabouts. How did Saul find out where to look for David? (22:6-9)

But instead of marching his entire army to Nob, Saul commanded all the priests to come to him. He accused Ahimelech of conspiring with David to put together a rebellion against Saul. How did Ahimelech answer? (22:13-15)

Ahimelech was truthful in his response. He knew little about David's real plans, because David had been evasive about his trouble with Saul when he talked with Ahimelech in Nob. Yet Saul wasn't convinced. What did he do? (22:16-19)

Only one person escaped Saul's judgment of the priests. Who was he? (22:20)

Who did David hold responsible for what had happened to the priests? (22:20-23)

The escape of Abiathar was very important to David because of what Abiathar took with him. The priests wore garments called ephods, and the high priest's ephod was special. On the breastplate of the ephod of the high priest were many precious stones, but two stones (called the Urim and Thummim) were very important and were worn over the heart. Somehow, the high priest could use these two stones to determine God's will in crucial situations. (See Exodus 28:15-30 and Numbers 27:18-21.) And when Abiathar escaped to join David and his men, he took the ephod with him.

Read 1 Samuel 23:1-29.
It wasn't long before David needed to consult God's will for a specific, sticky situation. What were the circumstances? (23:1-5)

David's initial fears had been justified. Because he had gone to fight the Philistines, Saul discovered where he was. But now that David had Abiathar the priest with him, he again sought God's will in the matter. What did he discover? (23:7-12)

What did he do? (23:13-14)

Notice that David's army is gaining strength. While hiding in the cave of Adullam, he had 400 followers (22:2). But now his numbers had already grown to 600 (23:13). Notice also that God was guiding both groups of people (David's group and Saul's group), so that they will not come into contact with each other. But another person found David and gave him some encouragement. Who was it, and what did he say? (23:15-18)

At one point, Saul's army was on one side of a mountain and David and his men were on the run on the other side. What prevented Saul from catching up with David that time? (23:26-29)

 JOURNEY INWARD

As you worked through this session, hopefully you noted how David handled **persecution and false accusations.** One question you may have is why David took such a defensive approach to the problem. You would think that anyone who could stand toe-to-toe with 9 1/2-foot Goliath armed only with a slingshot would have no trouble eliminating King Saul as well. Why do you think David chose to run rather than fight?

David probably had several reasons for trying to avoid King Saul. One of his major reasons becomes clear in the next session—David wanted nothing to do with harming a man whom God had anointed king over Israel. Sure, David knew he would eventually become king, but never did he assume that *he* had the right to take the life of the existing king. Another fact probably in the back of David's mind was that Saul had several sons, and one of them was his best friend, Jonathan. If David were to kill Saul in order to become king, something would have to be done about Saul's sons, and David probably didn't want to have to deal with that problem.

When you are persecuted by other people, do you tend to be a runner or a fighter? Why?

Think of any recent examples of persecution you have endured. Consider the following possibilities:

❏ Persecution because of unusual physical features
❏ Persecution because of unusual hobbies
❏ Persecution because of unusual mental abilities
❏ Persecution because of religious convictions
❏ Persecution just because people know they can bother you
❏ Persecution because of who your friends are

List any examples you can think of. Then for each example write down what you think motivates the other person's persecution. (Could those other people be jealous of you? Are they insecure about themselves? Maybe they just don't understand you, so they make fun of what they don't know. Perhaps they persecute *everyone*, and you shouldn't take their comments so personally.)

EXAMPLES OF PERSECUTION	POSSIBLE MOTIVES

No doubt David was aware that his persecution at the hands of Saul was the result of jealousy. He first tried to work out the problem, but when Saul's persecution intensified, David figured the best thing to do was just stay out of the way. God honored his decision by helping him stay one step ahead of Saul.

But even though David ran away to avoid conflict with the king, Saul still accused him of conspiracy. And David had to live as an outcast—a victim of false accusations. Think of the last time or two that you were falsely accused. What were the circumstances, and how did you react in each case?

After having reviewed David's patience during persecution and false accusations, would you react at all differently if the same circumstances occurred again? If so, how?

Keep your examples in mind. The next session will go one step further in offering suggestions for how to respond under these kinds of pressures.

 **KEY VERSE**
"Saul has slain his thousands, and David his tens of thousands" (1 Samuel 18:7).

How far should we go in resisting and fighting evil?

4

HIDE AND SNEAK

(1   S a m u e l   2 4 – 3 1)

Since World War II, a popular question for debate has been, "If you had had the opportunity to kill Adolph Hitler without getting caught or punished, would you have done it?"

Most people don't argue with the idea that murder is wrong. Yet when they weigh their beliefs against the fact that Hitler was a catalyst for racial hatred and was more or less responsible for the deaths of six million Jewish people, many people reconsider their attitude toward (and perhaps their definition of) murder.

Some never hesitate. They say, "I could pull the trigger with no feelings of remorse whatsoever." Others think they probably would have been *willing* to kill Hitler, but aren't sure they would have been *able*. Some justify their opinions because of the war conditions that existed. Still others hold to their beliefs that such an action would be murder under any condition, and therefore a sin they would not commit.

As human beings, we face a constant dilemma. We are to resist evil and fight it whenever we can. Yet we know that we will never completely eliminate it. And sometimes it's hard to tell just how far we should go to try to rid our lives of the influences of evil.

 **JOURNEY ONWARD**

Read 1 Samuel 24:1-22.

King Saul never exactly turned into a Hitler figure, but he was becoming more reluctant to accept God's will (to be replaced as king) and more determined to track down David. Toward the end of the last session, Saul's army had just about caught up with David and his men, but a Philistine attack forced Saul to return and defend his nation. He chased off the Philistines and quickly returned to his pursuit of David who now had about 600 men (1 Samuel 23:13). How many did Saul have? (24:1-2)

As things turned out, David found Saul before Saul found David. Through a divine "coincidence," Saul decided to take a "bathroom break" in the exact cave where David and his men were hiding. (David and his followers were deep in the cave while Saul remained toward the front.) What did David's men want David to do? (24:3-4)

What did David do instead? (24:4)

How did David feel about what he did to King Saul? Why? (24:5-7)

David followed King Saul out of the cave. How did David act as he confronted Saul? (24:8-10)

What did David do to show his sincerity? (24:11-13)

Getting Personal — *How do you show your sincerity to those who have wronged you?*

David suggested that King Saul let God settle the matter between them. He showed honor for Saul's position as king of Israel. And David said he was leaving his well-being to God. In other words, David knew that God had appointed him to be the next king. If Saul killed him right there, then God's promise to David wouldn't come true. Therefore, David felt pretty secure. (But the next step was up to Saul, a man who had already tried a couple of times to pin David to the wall with a spear.) How did King Saul respond to David's confrontation? (24:16-19)

What did King Saul say to indicate that he was aware of God's will for the future of Israel? (24:20-22)

After his talk with David, Saul went home. But David and his men returned to a stronghold. Why do you think David and his men didn't go back with Saul?

At this time in Israel's history, Samuel died. His death and burial are described in a single verse, because it was through his life that he modeled God's righteousness and power. So his death is noted, and the biblical narrative continues.

Read 2 Samuel 25:1-44.
As David's men continued to wander around, they came close to the home of a couple whose shepherds and flocks they had previously protected. How would you describe the couple? (25:1-3)

David sent 10 of his men to ask the man (Nabal) for whatever provisions he could spare. How did Nabal respond to David's request? (25:9-11)

Getting Personal – *Are you always kind and helpful when people come to you for help? Why or why not?*

David was angry. He even took two-thirds of his army and went with the intention of killing Nabal and everyone who worked for him. He felt like he had been treated unjustly (which he had) and that he had the right to "settle the score." But something happened to prevent David from carrying out his initial intentions. What was it? (25:14-35)

Abigail wasn't quite as dense as Nabal. She recognized that David was fighting God's battles and that he had every right to ask for help from the people in the area. And David didn't see Abigail as a meddling wife—he saw her as a messenger from God indicating that he should back off from his intentions to kill Nabal. David ended up learning a valuable lesson about revenge. What happened shortly after David decided not to kill Nabal? (25:36-39)

What did David do after he witnessed God's judgment on Nabal? (25:39-42)

In addition to Abigail, David had married a woman named Ahinoam. You may also remember that he had married Michal, the daughter of King Saul. But when David fell out of favor with Saul, the king gave Michal to another man to marry (25:44).

Round Two
Read 1 Samuel 26:1-25.
After David spared Saul's life and Saul returned home, it didn't take him long to change his mind about wanting to capture David. Saul took his 3,000 men with him again to begin another manhunt. But it wasn't too easy for that many people to remain inconspicuous. David soon discovered where Saul's army was camped, and that night he took a guy named Abishai with him to check out Saul's camp. And David had another perfect chance to get rid of King Saul. What were the circumstances this time, and why wouldn't David kill the king? (25:7-11)

What did David do instead of killing King Saul? (26:12)

Getting Personal – *If you had been David, would you have spared Saul's life? Why or why not?*

David couldn't resist a little taunting after sparing Saul's life this second time. He yelled out to Abner, the commander of Saul's army, and asked him why he wasn't doing his job of protecting the king. David told Abner to look for Saul's spear and water jug, and Saul's people realized that David again could have killed Saul easily. In all the commotion, Saul woke up, recognized David's voice, repented of his evil intentions, and went home again (26:13-25).

Read 1 Samuel 27:1-12.
David was no dummy. He knew it was just a matter of time until Saul changed his mind again about hunting him down. And he also knew that perhaps the next time they met, Saul might be the one who was awake, standing with the spear in his hand over a sleeping David. So David took his 600 men and returned to the land of the Philistines. He already knew King Achish of Gath (see 21:10-15), and he also assumed that King Saul would never pursue him into the land of the Philistines. Was David right? (27:4)

In spite of the advantages of living with the Philistines, David also faced some obvious disadvantages. King Achish let David live there because he figured that David would help him fight against the Israelites. Achish mistakenly assumed that since David wanted to stay away from King Saul, he must not be loyal to Israel. David benefited from the Philistine king's ignorance, so what did David request to put a little distance between his men and King Achish? (27:5-6)

David and his men spent their days raiding enemies of the Israelites to the south (the Geshurites, the Girzites, and the Amalekites). But they would tell King Achish that they were raiding Israelite towns. And to ensure that their deception was not discovered by the Philistines, they had to make certain to kill everyone in the towns they attacked. Meanwhile, they began to accumulate flocks and other goods from the cities they defeated. What did

Achish think about all David's efforts? (27:12)

Read 1 Samuel 28:1-25.
But then the Philistines began to put together an army to march against Israel. This caused problems for both David and King Saul. Since King Achish trusted David, he naturally assumed that David would fight with the Philistines against the Israelites (the nation for which David had been anointed to be the next king). David wasn't quite ready to be completely truthful with King Achish, so what did he tell him? (28:1-2)

And King Saul's problem was even worse than David's. He had fought and defeated small raiding parties of Philistines who had come into Israel, but when he saw his enemies united against him, he was filled with terror. He tried to find out what God wanted him to do, but he could get no answer. Previously, he would have run to Samuel for help, but now Samuel was dead. In his desperation, what did King Saul do? (28:4-8)

Getting Personal — *What kinds of similar occult practices are evident today in your community?*

Saul's actions were in defiance of his own law. He had previously outlawed occult practices in Israel, and had expelled all such people from the land (28:3). The woman he visited knew she was violating the law and was hesitant to work for people she didn't know, probably because she feared that someone might turn her in to King Saul. She wouldn't do anything until Saul (in disguise) promised that no harm would come to her (28:9-10). Whose spirit did Saul want the woman to contact? (28:11)

What happened when the woman tried to do what Saul had asked? (28:12)

This passage raises a lot of questions. Exactly how did the woman operate? Did she use black magic to contact demons who represented the people she was asked to reach, or did she use some kind of trick to make people think she was actually contacting the dead? And why was she so frightened during this experience? Did God allow the actual spirit of Samuel to appear to the woman? And just how was she able to recognize that her disguised visitor was actually King Saul?

The answers to most of these questions may be debated for years to come. But in any case, the Lord spoke to Saul through this image of Samuel and gave him a truthful prophecy. What did King Saul discover about his upcoming battle with the Philistines? (28:13-19)

How did King Saul respond to the news? (28:20-25)

David's Dilemma
Read 1 Samuel 29:1-11.
Meanwhile, David was continuing to face his own problems. He was caught between the proverbial rock and a hard place. To refuse to go to battle with the Philistines would reveal his loyalty to Israel and place his men in a dangerous position. Yet if he marched with the Philistines and was seen by his fellow Israelites, what would they think? And David and his men were in the back of the Philistine ranks. It would be difficult for them to turn against the Philistines during the battle because they would be cut off and unable to "make a run for it" back to the Israelites. And even if they tried, who knew whether King Saul would welcome them back or take the opportunity to kill them once and for all. What happened to keep David from having to decide what to do? (29:1-7)

David acted disappointed when King Achish gave him the "bad" news. David asked Achish, "Why can't I go and fight against the enemies of my lord the king?" (29:8) Whom do you think David was referring to as "my lord the king"—Achish, Saul, or God?

Read 1 Samuel 30:1-31.
But with this crisis solved, David soon discovered he had additional problems. When he and his men returned to their city of Ziklag, what did

they find? (30:1-5)

You need to remember that David's "army" at this time was actually a group of outcasts who, like him, were on the run from King Saul and the authorities of Israel (22:2). And when they faced this crisis, some of them began to talk of stoning David. Yet David responded to this problem the same way he did to any problem—he asked God what to do. What did God tell David to do? (30:6-8)

Two hundred of David's men were too exhausted to go with the rest of the army, so David left them behind to guard their supplies. As the rest of David's men pursued the Amalekites who had burned their city, they found an Egyptian servant who had been deserted by the raiding party. He showed them where the Amalekites were camped, and a battle followed. What were the results of the battle? (30:16-20)

When David and the 400 men who had gone with him returned to the camp where the other 200 men were waiting, some of the 400 tried to make trouble. What was their complaint, and how did David settle it? (30:21-25)

David realized that it was God who allowed him to recover what had been taken from him. So he took some of the goods his men had taken from the Amalekites, divided it, and sent gifts to his loyal friends and the people who had helped him as he was running from King Saul.

Read 1 Samuel 31:1-13.
David probably didn't realize how close he was to becoming king of Israel, but the day after King Saul visited the medium at Endor, he died in the battle with the Philistines. What were the circumstances of King Saul's death? (31:1-6)

What happened to the bodies of Saul and his sons after they died? (31:8-10)

You may not remember the location of Saul's first action as king. But if you review the facts of 1 Samuel 11:1-11, you should be reminded that the people of Jabesh Gilead were threatened by an Ammonite king who intended to gouge out the right eye of every man in the town. King Saul rescued the town and defeated the Ammonites. Now the men of Jabesh Gilead had an opportunity to return the favor. Saul had prevented them from suffering the humiliation of the Ammonites. What did they do to reduce Saul's humiliation at the hands of the Philistines? (31:11-13)

 JOURNEY INWARD

David's actions in this session are an outstanding example to follow as we examine our own lives and our attitudes toward **patience and revenge.** In the New Testament, patience is listed among the fruit of the Spirit (Galatians 5:22) because patience isn't usually a natural response to trying circumstances. When we are wronged, our first thoughts are usually how we can "get even." If we aren't tuned in to God's Spirit, revenge usually overpowers any patience we might be able to muster. David's actions toward Saul reflect a real spiritual maturity.

How about *your* spiritual maturity? Mentally put yourself in the following situations, and circle the appropriate number on the scale to indicate how you would respond (1 = Complete patience; 10 = Revenge with a vengeance).

A teacher unjustly accuses your child of cheating on a test.

1   2   3   4   5   6   7   8   9   10

The office gossip spreads lies about you, trying to ruin your good reputation.

1   2   3   4   5   6   7   8   9   10

Your neighbor's son breaks your picture window but lets another boy take the blame.

1   2   3   4   5   6   7   8   9   10

The first time you invite your date in for coffee, your dog suddenly forgets he's housebroken.

1   2   3   4   5   6   7   8   9   10

Your spouse ridicules your new haircut.

1   2   3   4   5   6   7   8   9   10

When was the last time you tried to take revenge on someone? What happened?

When was the last time you patiently decided to overlook someone's wrong actions toward you? What happened?

If we let God handle vengeance, we can be free to work on increasing our patience. Most of the time you'll discover that the best "revenge" is ignoring the person who is offending you. (It'll drive the person crazy.) After the person lives with his own meanness for a while, he or she will probably be in desperate need of a friend. If you've developed enough patience, you may have the opportunity to reach out to the person and restore the relationship (like David did with King Saul).

Take some time and think of three things you can do this week to increase your patience and decrease your desire for revenge. That part should be fairly easy. The hard part is actually doing them. But if you do, you may be surprised at how much better your life will be.

1.

2.

3.

 **KEY VERSE**

"May the Lord judge between you and me. And may the Lord avenge the wrongs you have done to me, but my hand will not touch you" (1 Samuel 24:12).

Everyone's life is sprinkled with mistakes.

5

LONG LIVE THE (NEW) KING!

(2 S a m u e l 1 – 1 2)

Much has been spoken and written through the years about mankind's tendency to make mistakes. Everyone's life is sprinkled with a generous assortment of failures, setbacks, mistakes, and shortcomings. Here are a few sample quotes by noted authors:

"Any man may make a mistake; none but a fool will persist in it" (Cicero).

"Had she not been mistaken, she would have accomplished less" (Ralph Waldo Emerson).

"I can pardon everybody's mistakes except my own" (Marcus Cato).

"The only things one never regrets are one's mistakes" (Oscar Wilde).

"The shortest errors are always the best" (Moliere).

"Love truth, but pardon error" (Voltaire).

"Truth is a good dog; but, beware of barking too close to the heels of error, lest you get your brains kicked out" (Samuel Taylor Coleridge).

"Who errs and mends, to God himself commends" (Cervantes, *Don Quixote*).

"If any man hopes to do a deed without God's knowledge, he fails" (Pindar).

By this point in your life, you've probably made enough mistakes to come up with some sage sayings of your own. But it seems that most people never really get comfortable with making mistakes. We would avoid them if we had the opportunity. But before we can avoid making mistakes, we need to know what causes them. So as you go through this session, look for sources of mistakes. During the **Journey Inward** section, you will have an opportunity to try to determine how you can eliminate some of the mistakes in your life.

 JOURNEY ONWARD

Read 2 Samuel 1:1-27.

The last session concluded with the death of King Saul and three of his sons. You should remember that Saul was wounded and then killed himself to avoid capture and possible humiliation by the Philistines. But as this session begins, a slightly different version of King Saul's death is given. Who was the "eyewitness" to Saul's death, and what was his story? (2 Samuel 1:1-10)

A couple of possibilities exist for why this guy's story didn't exactly match King Saul's. Perhaps he was telling the truth and had helped in some small way to assist King Saul in his suicide. But more likely, the guy saw an opportunity to try to impress the new king of Israel (by taking credit for killing the previous king). Another interesting fact is that this guy was an Amalekite, and David and his men had just destroyed the Amalekites for stealing their women and burning their city. Yet David took this Amalekite at his word and gave him what he thought the guy deserved. What did David do to the Amalekite? (1:11-16)

Read 2 Samuel 2:1-32.

David mourned for Saul and Jonathan, and then sought God's guidance for what to do next. God had David's group move to Hebron, a town in the center of the tribe of Judah (David's tribe). The men of Judah then gathered in Hebron to anoint David king over Judah. What was David's first official act? (2:4-7)

Getting Personal — *Put yourself in David's place. What would your first official act have been?*

But David's transition to king was not to be an easy one. Even though his own people in Judah recognized him as king, and God recognized him as king, several of the other tribes in Israel had other ideas. The commander of Saul's army was a man named Abner, and Abner wasn't ready to concede the kingship to David. (Perhaps Abner wondered about his future if he gave in to the man whom he had been fighting so hard against in recent skirmishes. Abner was also related to King Saul [1 Samuel 14:50].) So Abner found one of Saul's sons who hadn't been killed in the battle and named him king over Israel. The man's name was Ish-Bosheth. And for a while, Judah followed David while Israel followed Ish-Bosheth.

Then one day Abner suggested a contest (really a minibattle) between 12 of his men and 12 of David's men. He suggested this to Joab, the commander of David's army. Joab agreed, and the two teams met at a pool in a place called Gibeon. What were the results of the 12-against-12 contest? (2 Samuel 2:15-16)

Because the contest was indecisive, the competitive spirit of the men escalated into a full-scale battle between David's (and Joab's) men and Ish-Bosheth's (and Abner's) men. The fighting was fierce, and David's men were eventually victorious. Yet an event occurred during the battle that had personal significance to some of the leaders of the armies, and should be noted. Joab, the leader of David's army, had a brother named Asahel, who was determined to capture or kill Abner, the leader of Ish-Bosheth's army. Review 2 Samuel 2:18-23 and describe what happened.

After Asahel was killed, his two brothers (Joab and Abishai) continued to pursue Abner. But finally, Abner was able to convince Joab that their personal disagreement would get a lot of other people killed, so Joab gave up the chase.

War continued between David and Ish-Bosheth, and as it did, David gained in strength while Ish-Bosheth grew weaker. And as often happens when things are going badly, the people on the losing side began to argue among themselves. Abner had been trying to gather a following of his own, even while he was in charge of Ish-Bosheth's army. Apparently, there was some jealousy between the two men. At one point Ish-Bosheth accused Abner of sleeping with King Saul's concubine. It is unclear whether Abner was guilty of the charge, but by the accusation itself, King Ish-Bosheth was accusing Abner of trying to take over his command. (Sleeping with a king's concubine was like putting oneself on a level with the king.)

Read 2 Samuel 3:1-39.
Abner, angry with Ish-Bosheth, began to undermine the king and gather support for King David of Judah. Then Abner contacted David, offering to "jump ship" and bring Israel's support with him. What condition did David place on the agreement? (3:12-16)

Abner unmercifully obeyed David's request, and then made plans to convince Israel to support David from that point on. David prepared a feast for Abner and his men, and the plans were made. However, Joab was out of town while these plans were being made. When he returned and discovered that David was forming an alliance with Abner, Joab was angry. He accused Abner of spying on Judah and warned David that Abner didn't really mean what he was saying.

Then, without David's knowledge, Joab sent messengers to bring Abner back to Hebron. What did Joab do when Abner returned, and why did he do it? (3:26-27)

David made it clear that he didn't approve of Joab's actions. He went into mourning for Abner and wouldn't eat, even with the encouragement of his people. David's humility impressed the Israelites. Everything he did pleased the people.

Skim 2 Samuel 4:1–5:25.
Meanwhile, things just got worse for Ish-Bosheth. The news of Abner's death was alarming to him, but he didn't have long to worry about his future. What happened to him? (4:5-8)

How did David treat the two people who tried to gain his favor by eliminating Ish-Bosheth from the scene? (4:9-12)

In spite of all the action in David's life so far, he was only 30 years old when he was made king. And when he became king over Israel as well as Judah, he realized that it would be natural for the two separate divisions of the nation to be antagonistic toward each other. Consequently, he decided to establish his capital city in a territory that would cause neither portion of his realm undue jealousy. He chose Jerusalem, a fortified city located in between Israel and Judah. The only problem was that Jerusalem was at that time occupied by the Jebusites, but David attacked them and captured the city. Why was David so successful at everything he attempted? (5:9-10)

Getting Personal – *Have you known anyone similar to David who seems to be successful at everything? To what or whom do you attribute that person's success?*

The Philistines were a little concerned that David was gaining favor among the Israelites as well as the people of Judah, so they mounted an attack. The first time, God told David to fight them, and Israel was victorious. But in the second battle, God gave David a sign to wait for before moving ahead to fight. What was the sign? (5:22-25)

Read 2 Samuel 6:1-23.
When David had settled in Jerusalem, he decided to send for the ark of the covenant. But in transit, a tragic event occurred. What happened, and why? (6:1-7)

The Old Testament books of the Law were clear in their warning not to touch the holy things of God (Numbers 4:15). God's instructions were clear, and so were the consequences of what would happen to anyone who disregarded His instructions. In fact, God had designed the ark to be carried by poles on either side of it (Exodus 25:12-15). When the Philistines captured the ark, they didn't know any better and transported it on a cart. It seems the Israelites used the same method in this instance. If they had been carrying the ark in the manner intended by God, the tragedy to Uzzah would have probably been avoided.

David was crushed by what happened to Uzzah, and he refused to have the ark continue to Jerusalem. He had it stored in another man's house for three months instead. What happened to the man who took care of the ark during those three months? (2 Samuel 6:9-11)

When David was convinced that it was all right to continue the movement of the ark to Jerusalem, he praised God by dancing (6:12-15). David's wife Michal didn't approve of his creative expression of joy to God. In fact, "she despised him in her heart" (6:16). The linen ephod he was wearing was probably short, and perhaps his dancing may have revealed more of him than Michal thought was proper. Or maybe Michal was just embarrassed that her husband, the king of Israel, wasn't acting very kingly. What was the consequence of Michal's complaining? (6:23)

Skim 2 Samuel 7:1–10:19.
David's faithfulness to God over the previous years was rewarded. God gave David a period of peace, which gave him time to reorganize and think a little. And one of the first things David noticed was that he was living in a solid home of cedar while the ark was still in a tent, a "temporary" dwelling. David and the Prophet Nathan were discussing the accommodations of the ark, and David proposed to build a temple for the ark. Nathan thought it was a pretty good idea, and advised David to go ahead with the project. But during the night, God sent a message to Nathan. What was the message Nathan was to give David? (7:5-6, 9-13)

The eighth chapter of 2 Samuel is a "catch-up" chapter. It tells of several of the accounts of King David that had previously taken place, but had not yet been recorded. If you read through it, you will discover an unusual way to weed out enemies (v. 2), how David accumulated some of his nation's wealth (vv. 7-8), and other mini-stories that led to David's fame and success.

Another matter of business David wanted to catch up on was to see whether any of Saul's descendants were left, so he could show kindness to them. Why did David want to be nice to Saul's family? (9:1)

Who was found for David to honor, and how did he care for that person? (9:3-11—also see 4:4)

Taking care of Saul's descendants was just one thing David did to try to maintain good relationships with people he had known before becoming king. Another thing he did was send a delegation of his men to express sympathy when the king of the Ammonites died. The king had been good to David, and David wanted to continue a positive relationship with his son, the new king. But what happened when David's men reached the new Ammonite king with their message of sympathy? (10:1-4)

David was outraged when he heard of the humiliating treatment his men had received from the Ammonites. What did David do to prevent his men from suffering further embarrassment among their peers? (10:5)

When the Ammonites discovered how angry David was, they started hiring soldiers from several different locations to put together an army quickly. And when David heard about their army, he immediately assembled the Israelite army. A battle took place, Israel was victorious, and some of the nations that had fought for the Ammonites made peace with Israel and became subject to David (10:6-19).

A Sad Mistake
Read 2 Samuel 11:1-27.
You may not have noticed, but up to this point David's life has been practically mistake-free. He seems to instinctively stop and seek God's guidance whenever he faces a crisis, and God always gets him through the toughest problems and emergencies. But in 2 Samuel 11, David's near-perfect record is about to become stained. Review 2 Samuel 11:1-5 and answer the following questions:

❑ What sin did David commit?

❑ What was the result of that sin?

❑ Why do you think David committed that sin?

David decided to try to cover up his sin before anyone found out about it. What was David's first plan, and why didn't it work? (11:6-11)

What was David's second plan, and why didn't it work? (11:12-13)

David's third plan worked. What did he do to get rid of Uriah? (11:14-17)

Joab, the commander of David's army, was nervous even though he had followed David's instructions. He felt bad that more Israelite men had been killed in addition to Uriah. But David understood that in order for his plan to work, more people had to be sacrificed to cover his sin. He coldly chalked it up to the casualties of war.

Upon hearing of Uriah's death, Bathsheba mourned for a time. Then David married her, and she had the baby she had conceived during their affair. David thought his third plan had successfully fooled everyone. Had it? (11:27)

Read 2 Samuel 12:1-31.
God used a creative method to confront David with the truth of his sins. He sent the Prophet Nathan to David. What comparison did Nathan make to

point out David's wrongdoing? (12:1-4)

How did David react to Nathan's story? (12:5-6)

After David's enraged response, Nathan quickly responded, "You are the man!" Nathan also told David three different things God was going to allow to happen because of David's sin. What were they? (12:7-14, especially vv. 10, 11, and 14)

Getting Personal – *What kinds of things has God permitted to happen in your life because of your personal sin?*

All of Nathan's prophecies were eventually to come true, but his third prediction happened within a week. How did David act before his child died? (12:15-17)

How did David act after his child died? (12:18-20)

How did he explain the difference in his actions? (12:21-23)

David had been quick to sin, but he was also quick to repent. After God confronted him with the wrong he had done, David didn't try to make excuses or justify his actions. And even though he didn't want to accept God's judgment in the matter and tried to talk God into letting the child live, he accepted God's decision and worshiped Him when it was all over.

God blessed David and Bathsheba with another son. What was his name? (12:24)

Then David returned to the duties of being king. He turned his attention to fighting the Ammonites, and the Israelites captured a 75-pound crown of gold and precious stones that they placed on David's head.

Before we end this chapter, keep in mind that two of Nathan's prophecies have not yet come true. You'll have to wait till the next session to see what happens.

 JOURNEY INWARD

No doubt as you worked through this session, you noted several mistakes that various people made. But were you paying attention to the sources of those mistakes? As you go through this section, try to learn from the mistakes of other people so you won't make so many of the same ones yourself.

First think of the Amalekite man who ran to David to take credit for the death of King Saul. More than likely he was lying in hopes of earning a reward. Can you think of a time (or times) when you told a lie and it turned out to be a big mistake?

Even if the Amalekite was telling the truth and had somehow aided in King Saul's death, he was quick to try to profit from the misfortune of others. And his action was still fatal. Recall a time when you ignored someone else's feelings in order to insure your own comfort or advancement.

Ish-Bosheth, the son of Saul, made the mistake of opposing David's authority as the next king. (Both Saul and Jonathan had known that David was to be the next king of Israel; surely Ish-Bosheth knew as well.) The source of his problem was a rejection of and opposition to God's will. What mistakes have you made recently because you weren't considering what God wanted you to do?

Then there was Uzzah's incident with touching the ark of the covenant. His mistake was disobedience, even though his intentions were probably good. Sometimes you may be quick to try to excuse a sinful action. Can you think of a time when you disobeyed God and tried to justify your actions?

And of course, David's mistake was probably the biggest of them all. The source of his mistake—which eventually led to adultery and murder—was the refusal to curb his own selfish, sinful desires. From time to time we all want things we know we can't (or shouldn't) have. Can you think of examples from your life when nothing really mattered except what *you* wanted, and when those selfish feelings led to severe problems?

Don't get the wrong idea from these observations. Mistakes are a part of life. Everyone makes them, and we all can learn from our mistakes. But we can also save ourselves a lot of grief if we will learn to identify the sources of our mistakes and not experience any more costly mistakes than we have to.

So as you look back at the list of mistakes you have made recently, search carefully for the *sources* of your mistakes. Before moving ahead, spend some time in prayer and ask God to help you recognize bad choices in the future before they actually turn into costly mistakes. A little discretion early in your decision-making process can save you a lot of unnecessary turbulence.

This point is reemphasized in the next session. You will examine the life of a person who could have had a lot going for him, but instead chose to make a series of bad choices. And you will be reminded just how costly mistakes can be.

 KEY VERSES

"The Lord Himself will establish a house for you. . . . Your house and your kingdom will endure forever before Me; your throne will be established forever" (2 Samuel 7:11, 16).

71

*What image comes to **your** mind when you hear the word **rebel.***

6

GOOD LOOKS + BAD ATTITUDE = REBELLION

(2 S a m u e l 1 3 - 2 4)

What image comes to mind when you hear the word *rebel*?

❏ A handsome Civil War Southerner, dressed in gray, defending his home and family from the invading Yankees?

❏ One of the loyal colonial minutemen, rushing out in 1776 to fight off the British?

❏ The classic James Dean image—a young, tough guy with a fast car, a cigarette hanging out of his mouth, and the near certainty of an early death?

❏ A grungy soldier in a third-world country valiantly trying to overthrow the fat leaders who oppress the poor people?

❏ A free-spirited individual who defies all forms of authority?

At certain times, rebellion may be a proper course of action against injustice or cruelty. But our society tends to glamorize rebellion. We sometimes pride ourselves on being "rebels," even when our rebellion is rooted in selfishness, greed, or other less-than-noble emotions.

Perhaps one of the best ways to search ourselves for signs of rebellion is to see how we react when caught in a sin. For example, in the last session you saw David's great sin—his adultery with Bathsheba and his murder of Uriah to cover it up. You also saw that David was genuinely sorry for his sinful actions. And while God did not let David's actions go undisciplined, He forgave David's sin and gave another child to David and Bathsheba— Solomon.

If you look closely at Nathan's words to David (2 Samuel 12:9-12), you may be concerned that David's troubles aren't over yet. And if that's what you're thinking, you're right. David's sin had a short-range consequence (the death of his child), but it also had a long-range consequence. David's sin involved the destruction of Uriah's family, and God would allow David's family to experience turmoil of its own. As you go through this session, notice what happens when someone responds to sin with an attitude of rebellion instead of repentance.

 JOURNEY ONWARD

Keep in mind that David had several wives and concubines, who had borne him many children. David's oldest child was a son named Amnon. Another son, by a different wife, was named Absalom. Tamar was David's daughter— a full sister of Absalom and half sister to Amnon.

Read 2 Samuel 13:1-39.
What problem was beginning to form in David's family? (2 Samuel 13:1-2)

What advice did Amnon receive from his friend? (13:3-5) Was it good advice?

Describe what happened after Amnon acted on his friend's advice (13:6-14).

Notice Tamar's wisdom. She appealed to Amnon with a number of good arguments—both moral (v. 12) and practical (v. 13). But Amnon disregarded her pleas and used his strength to overpower and rape her. What do Amnon's actions after the rape tell you about his true feelings toward Tamar? (13:15-19)

It didn't take Absalom long to figure out what had happened to his sister, but he didn't say a word to Amnon. He just kept his hatred bottled up inside. Two years later Absalom had a chance to get even with Amnon. What were the circumstances? (13:23-29)

Getting Personal – *What evidences of dysfunction do you find in David's family? How are David's family problems similar to those of families today?*

Read 2 Samuel 14:1-33.
Because of Absalom's revenge on Amnon, he had to flee the country. David knew Absalom's actions had been wrong, but he mourned for his son every day (13:37). After three years, Joab wanted to bring Absalom and David back together. Joab hired a woman to tell David a story. What did she tell the king? (14:5-11)

When David had ruled on behalf of the woman's fictitious son, the woman pointed out that she had only been trying to parallel David's circumstances. She wanted David to see that a parent would naturally suffer if one son killed another, was not forgiven, and was sentenced to death (not only because the parent would lose a son, but a potential heir). David realized that Joab had put the woman up to her story, but he agreed to have Absalom brought back to Jerusalem anyway. However, two years went by and David still refused to see his son.

Absalom finally decided to ask Joab to intercede between himself and his father. He summoned Joab twice, but Joab wouldn't respond. How did Absalom finally get Joab to come? And what was the result of their meeting? (14:28-33)

Read 2 Samuel 15:1-37.
Absalom also had a lot of hair, which was a positive status symbol during his time. Every once in a while he would get a haircut, and the weight of his cut hair was 200 shekels (five pounds). Absalom decided he could use his good looks to his advantage. He built up his image by traveling around in a chariot preceded by 50 men running ahead of him. He began to spend his days near the entrance to Jerusalem talking to the people entering the city. He would listen to their comments and complaints. How would he respond? (15:3-5)

Before long, Absalom had a whole group of supporters. And after four years of this, he decided to rebel against his father, David. Absalom told David he wanted to go out of town to worship (at Hebron), so David naturally let him go. Absalom took 200 men of Jerusalem with him and secretly sent messengers throughout Israel to spread the rumor that he had become king in Hebron. As the word spread, many of the people supported Absalom. David, not knowing how much support Absalom had, decided to leave Jerusalem. (Perhaps he didn't want the city destroyed in a battle.) David left 10 of his concubines behind to take care of the palace and took the rest of his household with him.

Skim 2 Samuel 15:1–17:29.
The following events are described in 2 Samuel 15–17, and include several people. Absalom's conspiracy had divided the loyalties of the Israelites, and they began to take sides. Some of David's and Absalom's supporters are listed below. Look up the verses and record the role and responsibilities of each person.

David's Supporters
Ittai the Gittite—a leader of 600 Philistine soldiers (15:17-22)

Zadok and Abiathar—priests (15:24-29)

Hushai—one of David's advisers (15:32-37)

Ziba—servant of Saul, then Mephibosheth (16:1-2)

Ahimaaz and Jonathan—sons of Zadok and Abiathar (15:36; 17:17-20)

Shobi, Makir, and Barzillai—friends of David (17:27-29)

Absalom's Supporters

Ahithophel—David's former counselor (15:12, 31; 16:20-23)

Mephibosheth—Saul's grandson (16:3-4)

Shimei—a man from Saul's clan (16:5-13)

Amasa—a nephew of David (17:25)

David was wise in sending Hushai back to Jerusalem to give bad advice to Absalom. Even though Ahithophel had advised Absalom to follow David and do battle as quickly as possible, Hushai convinced him to wait and gather a large army first (17:1-14). How did Ahithophel respond when he discovered that Absalom wasn't going to follow his advice? (17:23)

Skim 2 Samuel 18:1–19:43.

As David and Absalom gathered their armies to do battle, David gave his troops special instructions. What were they? (18:5)

David's men won the battle, even though 20,000 men lost their lives. But losing the battle wasn't Absalom's biggest problem that day. What happened to Absalom? (18:9-18)

Joab sent word of Absalom's defeat to David. How did David receive the news that Absalom had died? (18:33)

How did David's response affect his men? (19:2-3)

David straightened everything out with his army, but was then faced with the same problem he had when he first became king—division in his kingdom. Absalom's army had just been at war with David's army, and now it was David's task to pull his nation together again. How did he try to reunite his people (based on the passages below)?

❏ 2 Samuel 19:13-14

❏ 2 Samuel 19:16-23

❏ 2 Samuel 19:24-30

But in spite of David's efforts to bring his nation together again, conflict persisted. The tribes of Israel had gotten into an argument with the tribes of Judah over David's return to Jerusalem. The men of Israel accused the men of Judah of not including them in the king's victorious return (only half of the Israelite army had had time to assemble). The men of Judah said it was no big deal—since David was from the tribe of Judah, they had every right to escort him home. The Israelites countered that they represented 10 tribes, and therefore should have had more involvement in the king's return.

Read 2 Samuel 20:1-26.
The conflict escalated until a man named Sheba saw an opportunity for personal gain. What kind of person was Sheba? (20:1)

What did he do to take control of the situation? (20:1-2)

David returned to Jerusalem to prepare for eventual combat with Sheba and his followers. David's concubines were there, and he assigned someone to take care of them. But since Absalom had slept with all of them, David arranged for them to live as widows (without sex) for the rest of their lives.

David then sent Amasa (who had replaced Joab as commander of the army) to gather an army in Judah within three days. But when Amasa had not returned within three days, David sent out the men he had under the command of Abishai, the brother of Joab. (Even though Joab was still with the army, David did not put him in command.) While David's men were pursuing Sheba, Amasa went over to greet them. What happened when Joab saw Amasa? (20:8-10)

With Amasa out of the way, the army rallied behind Joab and continued to give chase to Sheba. They caught up with him in a city called Abel Beth Maacah. The city was walled, so Joab's men built a siege ramp and were battering the wall to bring it down. But in the midst of all the commotion, a woman yelled to Joab and wanted to work out a solution rather than see her city destroyed. What agreement did they reach? (20:15-22)

With the problem solved, Joab and his men returned back to Jerusalem. Joab was again recognized as leader of the army. But don't forget about him. He'll come up again in the next session.

Skim 2 Samuel 21:1–24:25.
Chapters 21–24 of 2 Samuel are like an appendix that records events from the reign of King David, but not necessarily in chronological order. The first story is of a famine that lasted three years. David prayed to discover why God had allowed the extended famine, and God told him that Saul had previously "put the Gibeonites to death" (21:1). Nothing of this incident is mentioned elsewhere in the Bible, but apparently Saul had tried to wipe out this group of people whom the Israelites had previously sworn to spare.

Since Saul had never atoned for his sin against the Gibeonites, David approached them to see what action they thought would be fair to settle the matter. What did they request? (21:2-6)

David agreed to their request, which sounds harsh at first. Yet when you remember that Saul had tried to wipe out a whole tribe of people, the Gibeonites' proposal was not all that severe. Yet the effect on the seven men's relatives in Israel was tragic. Rizpah, the mother of two of the men who were handed over to the Gibeonites, mourned her loss in a major way. What did she do? (21:7-10)

When David heard of Rizpah's mourning, he collected the remains of the people killed by the Gibeonites, took the remains of Saul and Jonathan from the city of Jabesh Gilead, and buried them all together in Saul's father's tomb. After this incident, God ended the famine and again began to bless the land.

Second Samuel 21:15-22 records various highlights from some of David's army's past battles. As you read through this section, you'll find an agitated Philistine bearing down on an exhausted King David (and how God delivered him), some average everyday giants defeated by David's men, and one giant with six fingers on each hand and six toes on each foot. These events are recorded as a preface to 2 Samuel 22—David's song of praise to God. Much of this chapter appears in Psalm 18. Take a little time to compare the two and note David's tribute to God's protection.

David's praise to God continued throughout his life. His last official words are recorded in 2 Samuel 23:1-7. What did David have to say about:

❏ Righteous rulers?

❏ Himself?

❑ Evil men?

Second Samuel 23:8-39 records the exploits of some of David's best fighting men. What outstanding feat did each of the following men perform?

❑ Josheb-Basshebeth (v. 8)

❑ Eleazar (vv. 9-10)

❑ Shammah (vv. 11-12)

❑ Three unnamed men (vv. 13-17)

❑ Abishai (vv. 18-19)

❑ Benaiah (vv. 20-23)

But in spite of all the grand deeds of David's men, 2 Samuel ends on a negative note. God was angry with the Israelites, and again we don't know the exact reasons. In the meantime, David decided to take a census of Israel and Judah. The first verse of 2 Samuel 24 says that *God* told David to take the census, but the same account recorded in 1 Chronicles 21:1 says that *Satan* rose up against Israel and incited David to count his fighting men. The likely explanation is that Satan was the source of David's decision to take the census, but that God used David's action to bring judgment on the disobedient Israelites.

There appears to be little doubt that the census was sinful. Since there was no war at the time, Joab questioned David's motive (24:3). And after he had done it, even David knew he was wrong (24:10).

It doesn't seem like such a big deal to count the people in your army, but apparently this census was something of an ego trip for David. It may have been that he was receiving great satisfaction from being in charge of 800,000 Israelite warriors and 500,000 fighting men of Judah. Instead, he should have found his security in God.

Getting Personal — *Where do you look to put your security?*

When David asked God's forgiveness, God gave him three options. What were they? (24:10-13)

Which option did David choose, and why? (24:14)

David's choice of judgment resulted in the deaths of 70,000 people. But it could have been worse. Why? (24:15-16)

David actually saw the angel who was delivering the plague from God. And he knew the exact spot where the plague was stopped (just before the angel would have reached Jerusalem). David went to the owner of the land and made an offer to buy it and build an altar. What was the response of the owner? (24:22-24)

What did David then tell the landowner? (24:24-25)

The threshing floor that David bought on which he built his altar eventually became the site of the temple. But that's another story—one you'll get to in the next session.

JOURNEY INWARD

While this session has contained some positive stories, the majority of this portion of Israel's history is tainted by a prevalent attitude of **rebellion**. And this wasn't the "glamorous" rebellion mentioned in the introduction to this session. This type of rebellion was destructive and harmful—not only to the rebellious individuals, but to the entire nation of Israel.

It's not unusual to go through periods of rebellion. In fact, it's quite common. But hopefully, you have seen that rebellion can have severe, unexpected results. Rebellious attitudes that go unchecked can be deadly.

Think of a rebellious attitude you have—toward a spouse, a boss, a neighbor, or anyone else that comes to mind. (If you can't come up with a current example, think of one in your recent past.) Analyze your own rebellion as you review the ingredients and results of Absalom's rebellion.

Ingredients of Rebellion

(1) Anger/Hatred—Absalom didn't want justice for his sister's rape; he wanted revenge. His uncontrolled anger resulted in murder. In your rebellious situation, try to identify exactly whom you are angry at and why. Write your responses below.

(2) Impatience—Absalom's impatience became evident when he had Joab's fields burned when Joab wouldn't come see him. In your situation, how do you show impatience?

(3) Pride and self-conceit—Absalom was good-looking, and he probably knew it. He added to his looks a flashy chariot and a collection of groupies. And he used his charm to manipulate. You may not think you're attractive enough to manipulate other people. But one common element of rebellion is that the person thinks he knows something that the other person doesn't—and he takes pride in that assumption. In your personal example, what is the "bottom line" about which you think you know best?

(4) Lying/Deceit—Absalom tried to convince everyone he was looking out for their best interests when in fact he was looking out for his own. In your situation, are you being completely honest with the other person or are you trying to deceive that person in some way?

(5) Irreverence toward God—Absalom told David he was going to Hebron to worship. His lie was bad enough, but even worse was his flippant attitude toward spiritual things. God's model is servanthood, and rebellious people cannot be servants. In your rebellion, how are you disregarding God's wishes?

Results of Rebellion

(1) Continual division—Absalom's rebellion obviously severed ties between himself and his father. But as a result, division also was established between David and his army (Joab in particular) and between David and his people (Shimei, Sheba, and the Israelites in general). Does your rebellion affect people other than yourself and the person you disagree with? If so, how?

(2) Pain/Grief—Absalom probably didn't know how David grieved for him. His rebellious attitude completely devastated a loving father who had already forgiven him of murder. In what ways does your own rebellion affect the person it is directed toward?

(3) Eventual destruction—Absalom eventually died as a result of his rebellion. But lives aren't the only things that can be destroyed through

rebellion. Your relationships, self-image, and even your health can be wiped out if rebellious attitudes are allowed to fester inside you. In your situation, how is your rebellion having an effect on *you?*

Remember that many of these problems between David and Absalom were part of God's judgment of *David's* sin with Bathsheba. David's period of suffering would have been much more severe had he not confessed his sin and repented. The secret to dealing with rebellion is to get rid of it as soon as possible. Even though David had to suffer the consequences of his sin, he was restored to fellowship with God through his confession and God's forgiveness.

Take a few minutes now to reconsider your rebellious attitude. Be sure that God isn't pleased with it for a couple of reasons: (1) It doesn't set a good example for His kingdom, and (2) He knows your rebellion will eventually cause *you* to suffer in one or more ways, and He doesn't want that to happen to you. He wants what is best for you. So repent of your wrong attitude(s), seek or grant forgiveness wherever needed, and let God give you a fresh start. It's a hard step to take, but you won't be sorry.

 **KEY VERSE**

"O my son Absalom! My son, my son Absalom! If only I had died instead of you—O Absalom, my son, my son!" (2 Samuel 18:33)

What three wishes would you make?

7

STRAIGHT A'S IN WISDOM, BUT AN F ON THE FINAL

(1   K i n g s   1 – 1 1)

This is Aladdin's magical lamp. Rub it and make three wishes that you most desire. Write your three top wishes below.

Now an even more important consideration: Why did you choose those particular three wishes? Sometimes we wish our lives away, and never really consider *why* we want the things we want. If you're like most people, you used one or more of your wishes on things that would make your life easier or more comfortable—money, possessions, and so forth. Yet much of the joy in life is in the challenge of living it. If someone took away that challenge, you would miss many of the adventures of living.

Another thing to consider is how many of your wishes are short-term (dealing with immediate wants or needs) and how many are long-term (that would change the quality of your life over a long period of time). Some people, given three wishes, would spend them like a child in a candy store with a quarter. They would quickly get whatever they could, and the effects of their wishes wouldn't last long.

Now an even harder question: What if you had only one wish? Narrow your three down to the single thing you would wish for if you had the opportunity. Write it below.

And finally, if you knew someone was trying desperately to prevent your wish(es) from coming true, how would you feel?

 JOURNEY ONWARD

Read 1 Kings 1:1-53.

As 1 Kings opens, David is facing a situation where he has expressed his wishes, but is meeting opposition in having them fulfilled. He is old and ill, and the people of Israel are expecting a new king soon. (By the way, you should read 1 Kings 1:1-4 to see how people tried to keep the king warm in the days before electric blankets. And you'll need to refer back to this information later in the session.)

David had let it be known that he wanted Solomon to follow him as king, but another of his sons decided to try to claim the kingdom for himself. This son, Adonijah, was born after Absalom, but before Solomon. He also happened to be very handsome, and had not been disciplined much by his father, David. And apparently, Adonijah had learned some tricks from his older brother, Absalom. After deciding he wanted to be the next king, Adonijah gathered chariots and horses and 50 men to run in front of him.

Adonijah gathered support from many of the nation's leaders who had supported David—including Joab, the leader of the army, and Abiathar, one of the priests. Then Adonijah threw a big party for his followers (and brothers). They offered sacrifices outside of Jerusalem and apparently crowned Adonijah king (1:25). But Adonijah didn't invite Nathan the prophet or Solomon (1:10). Why do you think he left them off his guest list?

Nathan had received word of what was going on, so he went to see Bathsheba (Solomon's mother). The two of them knew that God intended Solomon to be the next king, so they worked out a plan to confront King David. Bathsheba was to go before David first and explain what Adonijah was doing, and Nathan would enter while she was still talking and back her up. Upon hearing their requests, David immediately made plans to anoint and announce Solomon as the next king. Was Solomon a popular king? (1:39-40)

How did Adonijah react to the news that Solomon had officially become king? (1:49-51)

How did Solomon treat Adonijah? (1:52-53)

Read 1 Kings 2:1-46.
Soon after Solomon was made king, David died. But first David left Solomon some advice and some instructions. David's advice was for Solomon to do everything God had commanded, and thereby prosper. According to the passages below, what instructions did David give?

❏ 1 Kings 2:5-6

❏ 1 Kings 2:7

❏ 1 Kings 2:8-9

Getting Personal – *What instructions for success has God given you?*

Apparently David had lived with certain dissenters in his kingdom (and had overlooked their previous wrongdoings). But he may also have suspected that such people would only cause grief for a new, less experienced king. Joab and Shimei were still guilty of their previous sins against David, but neither one had ever been "sentenced." So before David died, he decided to have Solomon carry out the sentence due them. (See Exodus 22:28 for the law broken by Shimei. Also review Joab's sins against Abner [2 Samuel 3:26-27] and Amasa [2 Samuel 20:9-10].)

Before Solomon could get around to carrying out David's instructions, he discovered some additional problems of his own. His half brother, Adonijah, who had already tried to take over the kingdom, went to Solomon's mother with a request. What was it? (1 Kings 2:13-18)

Adonijah's request seemed simple enough, but it probably carried a hidden motive. Abishag, the woman Adonijah wanted to marry, was the one who had been selected to sleep with King David and try to keep him warm in his old age. Solomon knew that an intention to sleep with or marry one of a king's concubines was a subtle statement that the person was able to fill the king's shoes. (Remember Absalom's actions in 2 Samuel 16:20-22?)

Solomon had already forgiven Adonijah for his previous uprising. What did Solomon do this time? (1 Kings 2:22-25)

With Adonijah out of the way, Solomon turned his attention to carrying out David's previous instructions. What happened to Joab? (2:28-35)

What happened to Shimei? (2:36-46)

Skim 1 Kings 3:1-28.
After Solomon had carried out all of David's instructions, he was ready to begin his reign as king. One of his first recorded acts is an offering to God. In fact, Solomon offered 1,000 burnt offerings to God (3:4). What did God do in response to Solomon's offerings? (3:5)

What did Solomon ask God for? (3:6-9)

Getting Personal – *Put yourself in Solomon's place. What would you have asked God for?*

What did God promise to give Solomon? (3:10-15)

It wasn't long before Solomon had the opportunity to have his wisdom challenged. A disagreement was brought before him to be settled. What were the circumstances? (3:16-22)

How did Solomon settle the disagreement? (3:23-27)

Read 1 Kings 4:1-34.
After seeing Solomon in action, the Israelites were awestruck by his wisdom and recognized that it must come from God. Solomon's kingdom was large and peaceful, and his people were numerous. He established governors and officials to help him rule. To get some indication of the extent of the lifestyle and number of rulers at this time, review 1 Kings 4:22-23 and write down what it took to feed Solomon's staff for one day.

Solomon's reputation as a wise ruler continued to grow. In what ways was his wisdom evident? (4:29-34)

A House for the Lord
Read 1 Kings 5:1-18.
Since Solomon didn't have to turn his attention to fighting battles, he had a lot of free time on his hands. What project did he decide to undertake? (5:1-7)

Solomon was on good terms with a king named Hiram, who gladly agreed to supply the wood for Solomon's new project. Hiram was from a place called Tyre, which was many miles north of Jerusalem. How did he plan to transport the wood? (5:9)

What kinds of wood did Hiram supply for the temple? (5:8)

With the supplies on the way, Solomon turned his attention to putting together construction crews. How did he get men to work on the temple? (5:13-14; 9:20-23)

Besides the people who worked with the wood, what kinds of craftsmen did Solomon recruit? (5:15-18)

Read 1 Kings 6:1-38.
The main part of the temple was 90 feet long, 30 feet wide, and 45 feet high. In front of the temple was a porch and around the temple were a number of side rooms. The construction of the temple was a little unusual compared to building sites today. What was different about the building of the temple? (6:7)

Getting Personal — *Suppose you were building the temple. What kind of architecture and furnishings would you use?*

The main hall inside the temple was covered in cedar so that no stones showed through. The cedar was carved and decorated with gourds and flowers. But the most holy place—the place there the ark of the covenant was kept—was more special. Describe the room where the ark was to be kept. (6:16-22)

What was inside that particular room? (6:23-28)

The completed temple probably looked something like this:

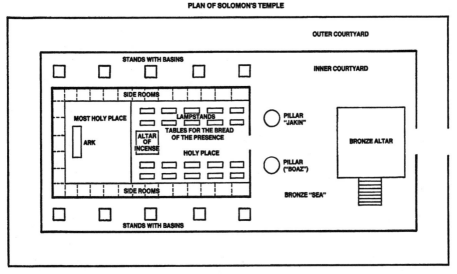

PLAN OF SOLOMON'S TEMPLE

How long did it take for Solomon to build the temple? (6:38)

After the temple was completed, Solomon decided to build a new home for himself. His palace was 150 feet long, 75 feet wide, and 45 feet high, and it took almost twice as long to build as the temple. In addition to the living quarters, the palace also contained a "Hall of Justice" in which Solomon would hear cases and act as judge.

Read 1 Kings 7:1-51.
When the buildings were complete, Solomon's next task was to see that they were properly furnished. He again recruited a person from Tyre to help him. This man's name was Huram (not to be confused with Hiram, the king of Tyre [5:1]). Huram's specialty was working with bronze. What furnishings did he make for the temple? (7:40-45)

Solomon didn't attempt to measure the weight of the bronze to determine the total value. Why not? (7:47)

The temple also contained an assortment of gold furnishings. What were they? (7:48-50)

If you recall the furnishings of the tabernacle in the wilderness, you'll note a lot of similarity between those objects and the ones in Solomon's temple. For instance:

❑ The ark of the covenant	1 Kings 8:6	Exodus 25:10-22
❑ Golden lampstand(s)	1 Kings 7:49	Exodus 25:31-40
❑ The altar of incense	1 Kings 7:48	Exodus 30:1-10
❑ The table for the bread of the Presence	1 Kings 7:48	Exodus 25:23-30
❑ The bronze basin	1 Kings 7:23-26	Exodus 30:17-21

After the temple was complete and furnished, Solomon called an assembly of the people. First the priests installed the ark in the temple. By this time, the only contents of the ark were the two stone tablets that God had given Moses. What other things had been kept in the ark? (Hebrews 9:4)

Skim 1 Kings 8:1-66.
During this time everyone was thankful, and so many sheep and cattle were sacrificed that they couldn't be counted (1 Kings 8:5). God was pleased, and He made His presence known. How? (8:10-11)

Yet Solomon was aware that God could not be contained by the heavens—much less any building. Solomon knew that the temple functioned more for the people to remember the presence of God than for God to have a specific place to live. What were some of the specific instances Solomon listed when people might need to seek the presence of God in the temple? (8:31, 33, 35, 37, 44)

After a prayer, Solomon dedicated the temple. What was offered to God that day? (8:62-63)

Read 1 Kings 9:1-28.
The dedication was part of a two-week festival, after which the people went home joyful. Later God again appeared to Solomon and reminded him of the importance of remaining faithful. What did God promise Solomon if he would continue to obey Him? (9:4-5)

What did God warn Solomon would happen if Solomon began to worship other gods? (9:6-9)

Getting Personal — *Are there other "gods" in your life? If so, what are they?*

Skim 1 Kings 10:1-29.
As Solomon continued to worship God, his wisdom and wealth continued to flourish. In fact, word spread throughout the earth. The queen of Sheba (Sheba is thought to have been located in what today is the southern part of Arabia) decided to see for herself what kind of ruler Solomon was. She put together a large caravan and traveled to Jerusalem to quiz Solomon with some tough questions that were on her mind. And Solomon answered all her questions. She said that even though she had heard much about the extent of Solomon's success, she had not heard even half of what was actually true. After trading gifts with Solomon, the queen of Sheba returned to her own country. Review 1 Kings 10:14-29 and write down some of the things that might have impressed the queen of Sheba about Solomon's reign.

Solomon's Downfall

Read 1 Kings 11:1-43.

As you read through the facts of the life of Solomon, you probably think that this was one person who really had everything he could have wanted. You see everything he had going for him and you expect a happily-ever-after ending. After all, on several occasions Solomon had been promised continued success as long as he remained faithful to God's commands.

But Solomon had one weakness that outweighed his many strengths. What was it? (11:1-2)

How common was this weakness? (11:3)

How did this weakness affect Solomon's later life? (11:4-13)

Because of his unfaithfulness to God, Solomon found himself with adversaries for the first time in his life. Two were people who had had grudges against David, and they resurfaced at this particular time. But a third one was the person God had determined would follow Solomon as king over Israel. Who was this person, and how did he discover that he was to become king? (11:26-40)

Solomon tried to kill his new adversary but was unsuccessful. After 40 years of leadership, Solomon died. The story of his demise from World's Greatest Ruler to World's Greatest Failure is one of the most tragic in the Bible. For a man who once had so much, the account of his last days and death is surprisingly unspectacular.

 JOURNEY INWARD

This session's look at the life of Solomon contains some clear lessons in **evaluating success**. Before you go any farther, take a few minutes to rate your own success in the following areas. Put an "X" on the line where you would rate your current level of success.

CAREER

WRETCHED_____SHINING
FAILURE   SUCCESS

COMMON SENSE

WRETCHED_____SHINING
FAILURE   SUCCESS

SPORTS ABILITY

WRETCHED_____SHINING
FAILURE   SUCCESS

COORDINATION

WRETCHED_____SHINING
FAILURE   SUCCESS

APPEARANCE

WRETCHED_____SHINING
FAILURE   SUCCESS

RELATIONSHIPS

WRETCHED_____SHINING
FAILURE   SUCCESS

PARENTING

WRETCHED_____SHINING
FAILURE   SUCCESS

MARRIAGE

WRETCHED_____SHINING
FAILURE   SUCCESS

A lot of people today tell you that if you set goals and struggle as hard as you can to reach those goals, you'll eventually be "a success." But if that formula for success is correct, Solomon should be remembered as the Bible's greatest success story. Yet he failed as badly as (or worse than) we often do. Let's reconsider his life and see where he went wrong.

CONSIDERATION #1—*Was it God's will for Solomon to be a success?*
Sure it was. That's why Adonijah failed in his attempts to take over David's throne. Do you think God wants you to be a success?

CONSIDERATION #2—*Did Solomon begin his life with a genuine devotion to God?*
Yes. His desire for godliness and wisdom was stronger than his desire for money and fame. What are your greatest desires?

CONSIDERATION #3—*Did Solomon set goals?*
Again, yes. He built the temple and a new palace for himself. He expanded the boundaries of Israel. He developed trade policies that brought money into the kingdom. Do *you* spend your time productively, and are you willing to face new challenges?

CONSIDERATION #4—*Did Solomon continue his devotion to God throughout his life?*
Oops. That's where the great king went wrong. His devotion to women eventually overpowered his devotion to God. Is your love for anything (or anybody) else stronger than your love for God?

There's a lot you can do in your own power to become successful. But you can never truly be a success unless you place *obedience to God* above all other priorities. In fact, your very definition of success might change if you're willing to shift the emphasis from what *you* can do to what *God* can do for you. No other "secret" of success will work. Take Solomon's word for it.

 KEY VERSES

"*May the Lord our God be with us as He was with our fathers; may He never leave us or forsake us. May He turn our hearts to Him, to walk in all His ways and to keep the commands, decrees and regulations He gave our fathers*" (1 Kings 8:57-58).

Sometimes it's tough to find a successor.

8

WHEN TWO HEADS AREN'T BETTER THAN ONE

(1 K i n g s 1 2 – 1 9)

Iguess you all know why you're gathered here," said Wilson, the family lawyer. "You are all mentioned in Master Crawford's will, and as soon as the police are convinced that the death wasn't a result of foul play, we will need to be ready to divide up the estate."

At the mention of foul play, Raymond, the butler, looked a little nervous. But he nevertheless continued to pour the coffee.

Wilson continued: "To my oldest son, Biff, I bequeath my collection of rare butterflies and the train set he loved so much as a child."

"Is that *all*?" huffed Biff. "Why, I'm going to. . . ."

"To Clarisse, my impetuous daughter, I leave a trust fund of $200 a month— just enough for her makeup, I suppose."

"Two hundred measly dollars a month?" Clarisse screamed. "This estate is worth millions!"

Wilson ignored her. "To my younger son, Frankie, I leave bus fare to State University and the strong suggestion that he finally complete his education. He's going to need it." Frank winced.

"And to the butler, Raymond, the only person who ever did any work around here, I leave the balance of the estate: properties, cash, stocks, bonds, assets, cars, etc., worth in excess of $57 million."

"He's crazy," screeched Biff.

"Out of his mind," added Clarisse.

"Of course we're all going to contest," added Frank.

"I don't know. I'm rather satisfied," purred Raymond.

You've no doubt seen dozens of television shows that contained the previous scenario in some form. It seems that once someone becomes rich and prestigious, it is tough to find a successor for him.

Sometimes a star quarterback graduates from college, and the entire football team seems to fall apart. Or the enthusiastic president of a club moves away, and there seems to be no one else who can fill his or her shoes. Sooner or later, everyone is placed in the situation of having to live in someone else's shadow (or at least put up with some poor soul who's trying to live in someone else's shadow).

 JOURNEY ONWARD

This session deals with the problem the nation of Israel faced when Solomon died. If you remember toward the end of the last session, God had appointed a man named Jeroboam to rule after Solomon (1 Kings 11:29-31). But Solomon had named his son Rehoboam as successor (11:43). As you might expect, there is going to be a little conflict between Jeroboam and Rehoboam.

It doesn't take too long to figure out what kind of person Solomon's son (Rehoboam) was. As he began to take over for Solomon, the first thing the Israelites did was make a simple request of him. They reminded him of how hard they had had to work under Solomon, and promised that if he would lighten up a little, they would follow him faithfully.

Read 1 Kings 12:1-33.
Rehoboam decided to seek some counsel before answering the people. He first asked the older men who had previously given Solomon advice. What did the older group of people recommend? (12:6-7)

Rehoboam then consulted younger advisers that were his own age. What advice did they give? (12:10-11)

Getting Personal – *To whom do you go for advice?*

After listening to both groups of people, what did Rehoboam tell the Israelites? (12:12-15)

What did the Israelites do then? (12:16-20)

As the tribe of Judah rallied behind Rehoboam and the rest of the Israelites supported Jeroboam, the setting was right for a knock-down-and-drag-out civil war. What stopped it? (12:22-24)

Unfortunately, Jeroboam's character wasn't much (if any) stronger than Rehoboam's. It seems that Jeroboam was afraid that once the Israelites began to offer sacrifices in the temple, their loyalty would again return to the house of David (Rehoboam). What did he do to prevent that from happening? (12:28-33)

Read 1 Kings 13:1-34.
Jeroboam's action was a major step in leading his nation into idolatry, so God sent a man from Judah to confront the king. The man from Judah predicted a future time when a godly king named Josiah would clean up the improper worship practices begun by Jeroboam. What happened when Jeroboam tried to prevent the man of Judah from speaking? (13:4-6)

Jeroboam was then convinced that the man of Judah spoke for God, and he tried to get him to stay and eat. The man refused and started for home because God had told him not to eat, drink, or return home by the same route. But it happened that a local prophet heard what had happened at the altar at Bethel. He wanted to talk to the man of Judah, so he followed him. How did the prophet convince the man of Judah to go home with him? (13:15-19)

What happened because the man of Judah disobeyed God (even though he did so unknowingly)? (13:20-25)

The prophet who had lied to the man of Judah was sorry for the outcome of his lie. He went to where the man had been killed, took the body home with him, and buried it. (This is an odd story to find wedged in the history of the kings of Israel, but it shows the severe consequences of lying—especially when the lie is an intentional attempt to interfere with God's will.)

How did King Jeroboam respond to the warning by the man of Judah? (13:33-34)

Read 1 Kings 14:1-31.
Shortly thereafter, Jeroboam's son became sick. His son's name was Abijah (not to be confused with the prophet, Ahijah). Jeroboam told his wife to disguise herself and go to Ahijah to find out what would happen to their son. When you think about it, that was a pretty dumb idea. Jeroboam was

expecting to receive a message (through Ahijah) from God, but at the same time he expected God not to see through his wife's disguise. What happened when Jeroboam's wife went to see Ahijah? (14:4-6)

What did Ahijah tell her about Jeroboam? (14:7-11)

What did Ahijah tell her about her sick son? (14:12-14)

What happened when Jeroboam's wife got home? (14:17-18)

Divided Kingdom

In the meantime, the reign of Rehoboam (son of Solomon) wasn't going much better. Just as Jeroboam and the Israelites did evil, so did Rehoboam and the people of Judah. They set up worship places, sacred stones, and poles to foreign gods in many places. They even had male prostitutes that were connected to their false worship practices. Because of their lack of concern for proper religious procedure, God allowed Rehoboam's enemies to attack Jerusalem and carry off most of the valuable artifacts in the temple. And throughout their lifetimes, there was conflict between Rehoboam and Jeroboam. The united kingdom of Saul, David, and Solomon was now divided and would remain that way until after both the separate kingdoms were eventually defeated and carried into captivity.

Read 1 Kings 15:1-34.

By coincidence, Rehoboam's son was also named Abijah. (This was the name of Jeroboam's son who died.) Abijah followed Rehoboam as king. What kind of king was Abijah? (15:3)

Abijah was followed by his son, Asa. King Asa was different from the kings who had preceded him. What kind of king was Asa? (15:11-15)

Rehoboam, Abijah, and Asa were kings of Judah. While they were ruling, Israel also had a succession of kings. Jeroboam was followed by his son, Nadab. What kind of person was Nadab? (15:25-26)

Nadab was followed by a person named Baasha. How did Baasha become king? (15:27-30)

What kind of king was Baasha? (15:33)

Read 1 Kings 16:1-34.
Baasha was followed as king by his son, Elah, who reigned only two years. Why was Elah's reign so short? (16:8-10)

Elah was killed by Zimri, one of his officials. Zimri proclaimed himself king, and his first act was to wipe out all of Baasha's relatives (which fulfilled a prophecy concerning Baasha's and Elah's sins). But Zimri reigned only seven days. When the Israelites heard that Zimri had plotted and killed King Elah, they proclaimed the captain of the army (a man named Omri) king. Omri immediately attacked Zimri. What did Zimri do when he saw that he was going to be defeated? (16:16-19)

Omri didn't have the support of all the Israelites. Some of the people rallied behind another man named Tibni. But Omri's supporters were stronger than Tibni's followers, so Omri officially became king. Was Omri a good king? (16:25-26)

Omri was followed by his son, Ahab, who made quite a reputation for himself. How is Ahab remembered? (16:30-33)

As you have probably noticed by now, this period was not a high point in the history of Israel and Judah. It seems people were doing all they could do to go against what they knew should be done. One instance was the rebuilding of the city of Jericho. You probably remember Joshua's defeat of Jericho, but you may not remember that at that time a curse was put on the ruins of the city. Joshua said that anyone who rebuilt the foundations would lose his oldest son. And whoever set up the gates again would lose his youngest son (Joshua 6:26). But at this time in Israel's history, a man named Hiel rebuilt Jericho and lost two of his sons as a result (1 Kings 16:34).

A Courageous Prophet
Read 1 Kings 17:1-24.
But while the kings of the nations were weak and inconsistent, God called some prophets who stood strong and courageous. God instructed Elijah, a prophet, to go to Ahab and declare that Israel would receive neither rain nor dew for several years, until Elijah gave the word. After delivering the message, Elijah hid out and God fed him in an unusual way. How? (17:5-6)

Eventually the brook where Elijah stayed dried up because of the lack of rain. Elijah made friends with a widow in Zarephath, again under strange circumstances. How did Elijah come to stay with the widow, and how did God provide for them? (17:7-16)

Getting Personal – *Has God provided for you in any unusual ways? How?*

It was obvious that Elijah acted with the authority of God. One proof that he had God's power took place while he was still at the widow's home. What happened? (17:17-24)

Read 1 Kings 18:1-46.
Sometime during the third year without rain, God sent Elijah back to King Ahab to tell him that rain could be expected soon. On the way, Elijah ran into one of Ahab's officials named Obadiah—one of the few people around who truly believed in God. In fact, Obadiah had hidden 100 prophets of God and was secretly supplying them with food and water. Elijah greeted Obadiah and sent him to Ahab with instructions on where Ahab could meet Elijah.

When Ahab met with Elijah, it seemed that Elijah wanted to discuss the weakened spiritual condition of Israel before he wanted to talk about the weather. What did he command Ahab to do? (18:16-19)

When Elijah addressed the Israelites, he challenged them to follow the true God. He even told them to follow Baal if he could prove to be superior to Israel's God. But the people remained silent. How did Elijah suggest they determine which god was the true God? (18:22-24)

What happened during the "contest" on Mount Carmel? (18:25-38)

What effect did this demonstration have on the Israelites? (18:39)

The false prophets were then killed (according to Israel's laws). Elijah told Ahab to expect rain soon, and climbed on up Mount Carmel to pray for rain. What happened there? (18:41-44)

It's interesting to note how Ahab and Elijah got back to the king's palace. See 1 Kings 18:45-46.

Read 1 Kings 19:1-21.
If you were Elijah at this moment, think of how "pumped up" you must feel. The closest comparison we could make today would probably be winning the Super Bowl, the World Series, or Wimbledon. But if Elijah felt that way at all, his good feelings soon ended. As soon as King Ahab informed Queen Jezebel that her prophets were dead, she swore that the same thing would happen to Elijah within the next 24 hours. And Elijah—the same Elijah who had brought a dead boy back to life, had called down fire from heaven, had prayed for the return of rain after three years of drought, and had outrun a king's horse-drawn chariot over a distance of about 17 miles—panicked and ran for his life. But even while Elijah was on the run, God took care of him. How? (19:3-9)

At this time Elijah was convinced that he was the only prophet of God remaining. God was about to tell him that 7,000 true followers remained in Israel, but first Elijah needed to know that God was a God of the quiet moments (the fear of Jezebel) as well as the spectacular moments (like on top of Mount Carmel). How did God show that to Elijah? (19:11-13)

God told Elijah to return home, and He gave him some jobs to do. One of those jobs was to anoint a man named Elisha to succeed Elijah as prophet. Elijah did as God instructed (19:19-21), but the transfer of responsibility from Elijah to Elisha will have to wait until next session.

JOURNEY INWARD

As you've seen Israel split from one nation to two in this session, you've probably noticed a lot of issues that could be examined in-depth: change, weakness, failure, and so forth. But the one we want to focus on now is **courage.** In the last session you saw that success is obedience to God. Now you should see that courage is trust in God.

If Rehoboam and Jeroboam had been courageous enough to stand for God (instead of worrying so much about what other people thought), the divided kingdoms might have gotten off to a much stronger start. Instead, they both were led by a series of wimpy kings.

Elijah stood as a bold example of courage when he was outnumbered 450 to 1, but then he got to the point where one angry queen made him fear for his life. (Actually, it's sometimes comforting to remember that even the great heroes of the Bible had their weak moments.)

The first step in developing courage is identifying your fears. If you know what things to look for, you can better prepare to cope with them. Check all the fears below that apply to you.

PHYSICAL THINGS	PHOBIAS	INNER FEARS
❑ Spiders	❑ Fear of heights	❑ Fear that no one will
❑ Snakes	❑ Fear of closed places	(or does) like you
❑ Darkness	❑ Fear of water	❑ Fear of nuclear war
❑ Sounds at night	❑ Fear of open places	❑ Fear of being a failure
❑ Bugs (crawly things)	❑ Fear of flying	❑ Fear of dying
❑ Birds/Animals	❑ Fear of the dentist	❑ Fear of being alone
❑ Other_____	❑ Other_____	❑ Other_____
❑ Other_____	❑ Other_____	❑ Other_____

After Elijah admitted to God that he felt scared, alone, and ready to die, God spoke to him. But God didn't choose to address Elijah's fears in a powerful manner. Instead of appearing in a windstorm, earthquake, or fire, God spoke through a gentle whisper. Perhaps you're expecting or hoping for some kind of supernatural power to get you over your fears. But maybe you need to settle down and be able to hear God whispering, "Don't be so afraid. I'm right here." In fact, spend some time right now just to calm down and let God know what you are thinking about the fears you checked above. As you begin to trust Him, He will provide the courage you are looking for. And perhaps you will discover that He hasn't given you the power to overcome your fears so He can give you a better gift—the patience to endure them.

 KEY VERSE

"How long will you waver between two opinions? If the Lord is God, follow Him; but if Baal is God, follow him" (1 Kings 18:21).

Everyone tells a lie once in awhile.

9

PROPHETS AND LOSSES
(1 K i n g s 2 0 – 2 K i n g s 5)

Have you ever noticed that people don't like to admit that they are liars? Everyone tells a lie once in a while, but everybody also knows that telling lies is wrong. And in order not to let other people know that we are less than honest, we admit our untruths in other ways.

"OK, so I fibbed a little."

"There goes Stephen with another of his fish stories."

"Angela just can't seem to help but tell tall tales."

"It was just a little white lie."

"He stretched the truth just a little."

"She left out a few facts."

"Little Bethie exaggerates a lot."

"I hated her new hairstyle. I only told her I liked it so I wouldn't hurt her feelings—you know, to flatter her."

Truth isn't valued very much today. In fact, in some situations people have come to expect lies more often than truth. Most polls of students show that a large majority of them cheat regularly when they are convinced they won't get caught. Businesspeople are quick to point out that many résumés contain a number of lies that the applicant feels will help him or her get the job. And in many cases, even the personal references on the résumés are so exaggerated that they can't really be trusted.

Integrity is lacking in many of today's relationships. More than just a matter of truth vs. lie, integrity is a lifestyle of consistent, complete moral character. And where integrity is lacking, problems will arise. As you go through this session, look for examples where integrity is absent, and notice the results in each set of circumstances.

 JOURNEY ONWARD

You'll remember from the last session that the king of Israel at this time is Ahab—a classic example of someone lacking integrity. Ahab had some internal problems before, with the conflict between Elijah and the priests of Baal. But this session opens with an external problem that Ahab had to deal with.

Read 1 Kings 20:1-43.
A foreign king named Ben-Hadad put together a coalition and attacked Samaria (where King Ahab was headquartered). Ben-Hadad demanded the city's silver and gold, and the best of the women and children. Ahab agreed to this request, probably to avoid a battle and spare the city. But Ben-Hadad then revised his demands and insisted that his soldiers would come into the city and take whatever they wanted. Ahab would not agree to this second request. He and Ben-Hadad traded insults and the two parties prepared for war (20:1-12).

In spite of the evilness of King Ahab, God sent a prophet to inform him that he would win the battle so he would know the power of God. After the first skirmish, the Israelites beat back Ben-Hadad's army and pursued them, but Ben-Hadad escaped. The prophet of God informed King Ahab that Ben-Hadad would renew his attack the next spring, but that God would still deliver Israel. In the meantime, what excuse did Ben-Hadad use for losing the battle? (20:23)

The next spring, after Ben-Hadad had put together a new army, he again attacked Ahab. What was the result of the battle? (20:29-30)

With Ben-Hadad's army practically destroyed, King Ahab should have been quick to mop up any survivors—especially Ben-Hadad himself. But he didn't. Why didn't Ahab put Ben-Hadad to death? (20:31-34)

God sent a prophet to tell King Ahab that what he did was wrong. The prophet used a creative method to illustrate Ahab's lack of follow-through. How did the prophet show Ahab that he had made a grave mistake? (20:35-43)

Read 1 Kings 21:1-29.
Ahab's weak character is illustrated again in the following incident. Ahab was envious of a vineyard owned by one of his neighbors named Naboth. Ahab wanted to buy the vineyard from Naboth and make it a vegetable garden, but because the vineyard was part of Naboth's inheritance, he refused Ahab's offer. Ahab went home and pouted, refusing to eat. Queen Jezebel then took the matter into her own evil hands. What did she do to acquire the vineyard for Ahab? (21:7-16)

After Jezebel's atrocious actions, God sent Elijah to confront Ahab with a message. What was it? (21:17-19, 23-24)

At this point, the Bible repeats a point about Ahab made in the last session. What does it say? (21:25-26)

But as bad as Ahab was, he repented of his actions after he was confronted by Elijah. And God determined to postpone the destruction of Ahab's house until a later time.

Getting Personal – *How do you think your repentance affects God?*

Read 1 Kings 22:1-53.
While Ahab was king of Israel, the king of Judah was a man named Jehoshaphat. Jehoshaphat was basically a good king, but in this instance he was coaxed into an alliance with King Ahab to reclaim some land that was supposed to belong to Israel. What did Jehoshaphat request before he agreed to join forces with Ahab? (22:4-5)

At this time Ahab had 400 "prophets" he would consult before taking any serious action. But Jehoshaphat realized that they were not really prophets of God. Ahab knew of *one* prophet he could consult to hear what God had to say, but why didn't he like to ask him anything? (22:7-8)

At first, Micaiah the prophet told Ahab what he wanted to hear. But Ahab knew he wasn't being truthful. With further insistence from Ahab, Micaiah told him the truth. He said that God had tolerated the lying spirits of the other prophets so that Ahab would listen to them and go to his death in the forthcoming battle. How did Ahab reward Micaiah for his honesty? (22:26-28)

Ahab must have believed Micaiah's prophecy, but he engaged in battle anyway. Yet before he did, he took a precaution. What did he do? (22:30)

The enemy army had been given instructions to seek out the king of Israel and destroy him, regardless of other circumstances. When they saw Jehoshaphat, they assumed he was king of Israel (because of his nice clothes) and began to chase him. But when his pursuers got close enough to tell he wasn't Ahab, they gave up the chase. In the meantime, Ahab thought he was safe. What happened to change his mind? (22:34-35)

Ahab's death fulfilled Micaiah's prophecy. And the next incident fulfilled another person's prophecy about Ahab. Review 1 Kings 22:37-38 and 1 Kings 21:19. Explain the other prophecy that was fulfilled.

After recording the death of Ahab (king of Israel), the account in 1 Kings mentions King Jehoshaphat (king of Judah), but it is a summary. If you go to 2 Chronicles 19–20, you will get a much better picture of what kind of person Jehoshaphat was. His biggest fault seems to be that he made unwise alliances with several of the kings of Israel. But for the most part, Jehoshaphat is remembered as one of the best kings of the divided kingdom. He pleaded with the people to return to God, and he removed most of the places where worship of other gods was taking place. When faced with problems, he turned to fasting and prayer to determine what God would have him do. And God honored Jehoshaphat's faithfulness.

Getting Personal – *When faced with problems, what do you do to determine what God wants you to do?*

Read 2 Chronicles 20:1-30.
Describe the unusual battle won by Jehoshaphat.

Read 2 Kings 1:1-18.
But in spite of Judah's good spiritual and political position, Israel was still in bad shape. Ahab's son, Ahaziah, was no better than his father. His problems were compounded when he was injured by a fall at about the same time that Moab decided to rise up against Israel. Ahaziah wanted to know if he was

going to recover from his injury. Instead of seeking God's answer, he chose to send messengers to consult another god. But God sent Elijah to intercept Ahaziah's messengers. What message did Elijah give them? (1:1-4)

Ahaziah recognized from his messengers' description that the speaker had been Elijah. He decided to send a group of men out to bring Elijah back to the palace—probably in a foolish attempt to convince Elijah to take back what he had said. What happened to the men Ahaziah sent out? (1:9-15)

Elijah eventually returned with Ahaziah's men. When he got there, he only repeated the message God had given him, and Ahaziah then died.

Elijah "Retires"
Read 2 Kings 2:1-25.
Some time later Elijah realized that it was time to turn over his responsibility as prophet to Elisha. As you can tell by reading 2 Kings 2:1-6, Elisha was committed to Elijah and the work he was doing for God. So Elijah took Elisha across the Jordan River to say good-bye. They crossed the river in an unusual manner. How? (2:7-8)

Elijah offered to do a favor for Elisha before leaving. What did Elisha ask for? (2:9)

Elijah agreed to grant Elisha's request under what condition? (2:10)

What happened to Elijah next? (2:11-12)

It didn't take long for Elisha to show that he was indeed a capable successor to Elijah. How did he exhibit God's power in a similar manner? (2:13-14)

Several of the other prophets wanted to send out a search party for Elijah. Elisha told them it would be a waste of time, but when they insisted, Elisha told them to go ahead. After searching three days without finding anything, Elisha could just say, "I told you so" (2:18).

Several of the incidents that followed immediately also proved Elisha's ability to act with God's power. Review the following two passages and describe the events.

❑ 2 Kings 2:19-22

❑ 2 Kings 2:23-25

Read 2 Kings 3:1-27.
And Elisha, like Elijah, soon found himself involved in political and military matters. Another of Ahab's sons, Joram, was now king of Israel. He wasn't as evil as Ahab and Jezebel had been, but he was no poster child for niceness and purity either. The territory of Moab was supposed to be under Israel's control at this time, and the Moabites supplied Israel with sheep and wool. But the king of Moab rebelled against Joram and refused to deliver what he had agreed to. Joram did what his father Ahab and brother Ahaziah had done—he called on Jehoshaphat for support. He also recruited the king of Edom to help go against Moab.

Jehoshaphat was true to form. Before blindly marching into battle, he wanted to call on a prophet and see what God had to say. Elisha was in the territory, so the three kings called on him to come and advise them. What was Elisha's attitude toward the three kings? (3:13-14)

What did Elisha advise? (3:15-20)

What was the result of heeding God's message given through Elisha? (3:21-27)

Read 2 Kings 4:1-44.
But Elisha's job didn't involve only the bigwigs of Israel and Judah. He, like Elijah, had a strong personal ministry and cared for the people around him. One example was how he helped a prophet's widow who was having financial trouble. What were the circumstances, and how did Elisha help? (4:1-7)

Elisha also made friends with another woman and her husband. They decided to furnish a room on their roof for him so he would have a place to stay every time he was in the area. Elisha wanted to repay the favor, so he asked his servant, Gehazi, what the lady might like. Gehazi knew she didn't have a son, and would have no one to take care of her after her husband died. So Elisha told the lady she would have a son within the year, and his prediction proved true.

But after the son had grown a bit, he had a health problem. What was his problem, and what did Elisha do to help him? (4:18-37)

Other lifesaving accounts involved Elisha. One time he neutralized a poisoned pot of stew and prevented a catastrophe for a group of prophets (4:38-41). On another occasion he fed a large group of people with a small amount of bread, much like Jesus would do later with the loaves and fishes (4:42-44). But one of Elisha's best-known miracles involved the healing of a man with leprosy.

Read 2 Kings 5:1-27.
The man's name was Naaman, and he was a commander in an army that often went to battle against Israel. In fact, Naaman's wife had a young servant girl from Israel who had been taken captive. But the young girl knew

that Naaman's leprosy could be cured if he would go see Elisha. Naaman made the arrangements and went. What happened? (5:9-14)

Getting Personal – *Have you ever known anyone in a position similar to the servant girl who was able to share his or her faith with a superior? How can you share your own faith with those around you?*

After Naaman was healed, he was convinced that Elisha's God was the only true God, and Naaman wanted to give Elisha some gifts. Elisha refused to accept anything, so Naaman started for home. This should have been the end of the story, but it wasn't. Gehazi, Elisha's servant, saw an opportunity for personal gain. Review 2 Kings 5:19-24 and describe what happened.

What happened to Gehazi as a result of his greed? (5:25-27)

More of Elisha's life will be examined in the next session. But now it's time to stop and see what you've learned (if anything) from this session.

 JOURNEY INWARD

Specifically, let's spend some time thinking about the importance of **honesty**. How important are honesty and integrity to you? Before you answer, think through your actions over the past two days. Retrace your steps from your first words in the morning ("OK. OK. I'm getting up"—when you really weren't) to your last words at night ("Sure, I'll take out the garbage"—when you have no intention of doing so). Make a list of any words or actions that reflect a lack of integrity. Look for the following things:

❑ Verbal untruths (or half-truths)
❑ Broken promises
❑ Hypocrisy (Actions that cause others to assume you're a good, moral person when they might not do so if they knew you better)
❑ Prejudices (Attitudes that cause you to treat other groups of people unfairly)
❑ Other problem areas that come to your mind

List any offenses below. (Give this some real thought, and be honest with yourself.)

In many instances, it's a lot easier to be dishonest than honest. Sometimes a lie seems to be the easiest way out of an uncomfortable situation (even though a lie is usually hard to keep straight after it has been told). When you look back at this session, you'll see that the Prophet Micaiah was imprisoned for his honesty. And even today, the results of telling the truth aren't always what we might wish for.

Yet, it is also important to observe the consequences of *not* telling the truth. Sure, it might have been hard for Gehazi to pass up a sure opportunity to make some quick cash, but it was even harder for him to live with the consequences of his dishonesty—leprosy. And while Ahab seemed to profit from his wife's framing of Naboth, his evil deeds finally caught up with him.

For each of the things you listed previously, think of the possibilities of what bad things *could* happen as a result of that action. (Of course, it is unlikely that every bad thing you listed will actually occur, but some of them will eventually catch up with you. It's important to occasionally envision what could happen if you don't try your best to maintain an honest lifestyle. As you begin to realize what *might* happen, you sometimes try a little harder to stay honest.) Number your answers above, and in the space below put the same numbers followed by the possible consequences of each of the previous things you listed.

This exercise should have been a little uncomfortable for you. You see, it's important to consider the possible consequences of our dishonesty. But that's not the *best* way to cultivate honesty; it's the back door to integrity. We shouldn't desire to be truthful people because of the bad things that may happen to us. If those potential problems get your attention, fine. But the best reasons for always telling the truth are because you want to and because God expects it of you.

No doubt you're thinking that you already know all this. If that's true, you shouldn't have been able to list any untruths in the previous section. So before continuing, think through the following questions:

❑ Do you honestly try to tell the truth *all* the time?
❑ Are you motivated to tell the truth because you might get in trouble otherwise, or because you really want to tell the truth?
❑ What dishonest habits can you begin to change *this week?*

And as usual, if you really want to improve your lifestyle, God will give you the strength and ability to do so. Honest!

 KEY VERSE
"Now I know that there is no God in all the world except in Israel" (2 Kings 5:15).

DON'T PANIC!

10
WHAT'S YOUR BIG WORRY?
(2 K i n g s 6 – 1 0)

Douglas Adams, in his series of science fiction books, describes a book called the *Hitchhiker's Guide to the Galaxy*. And he writes that one of the best-liked attractions of the book is the inscription on the cover. Every book cover contains the words, "Don't Panic."

Most of our lives would go a lot easier if we lived by the slogan, "Don't panic." But few, if any, of us lead a panic-free life. Instead, we worry. Think about the past 24 hours. What have you worried about? Work? Family turmoil? Relationships with other people? The possibility of being nuked if you don't mow that waist-high lawn? A prominent fever blister?

Worry is one of our biggest time wasters. According to statistics, only about 10% of the things we worry about actually come to pass. Yet we are conditioned to fret and fume and daydream of the worst thing that could possibly happen to us. And many times our periods of worry make life miserable for us. When faced with negative situations, we panic. We don't think; we panic. We don't look for ways around our problems; we panic.

In this book, you've probably noticed by now a difference between the kings and the prophets that you've read about. When things go wrong, the kings (with a few exceptions) are quick to panic. The prophets, on the other hand, assume that God is going to take care of the matter, and they just kind of wait until He gives them word on what action to take.

The kings we've seen so far have schemed against each other, burned down palaces on themselves, sought information from mediums and false gods, and acted in various other worrisome manners. A prophet gets hungry? God sends ravens to carry him bread. A prophet gets weak? An angel gives him a meal that gives him strength to last 40 days. A prophet is asked to heal a leper? Done! A prophet is outnumbered 450 to 1? No problem. God rains down fire from heaven to convince the people to follow the 1 and kill the 450.

For the most part, the prophets were able to see bad circumstances from God's point of view, and they could remain at peace even in turbulent times. The kings, for the most part, saw their own limitations, and they panicked under pressure.

 JOURNEY ONWARD

In the last session, you saw that Elisha was a man of integrity. In this session, notice that he was also a man of peace. That's not to say that he avoided conflict or stayed away from trouble, but he seemed to remain calm no matter what happened to him. You've already seen him act in a number of situations, and he's by no means finished yet.

Read 2 Kings 6:1-33.
Elisha is to be admired because people could approach him with problems that weren't exactly earthshaking or spiritually centered. For instance, review 2 Kings 6:1-7 and describe the miracle that Elisha performed.

Yet, at other times Elisha's demonstrations of God's power *did* have a national impact. For example, the king of Aram was at war with Israel, and Elisha was acting as adviser to the king of Israel. Every time the Arameans would set up a surprise attack on the Israelites, Elisha would alert the king of Israel and he would stay away from that particular area. After this happened a number of times, the king of Aram accused his officers of having a spy among them. How did they answer him? (6:11-12)

When the king of Aram discovered that Elisha was the one who was thwarting all his military strategies, he determined to capture Elisha. He sent men to find the prophet, and his men found Elisha in a city called Dothan. The king of Aram sent a strong force to Dothan during the night, and they surrounded the city. Elisha's servant got up early the next morning, saw the city surrounded with horses and chariots, and yes, he panicked. But when he ran to tell Elisha, the prophet remained calm. How did Elisha show his servant that things weren't really as bad as he thought they were? (6:15-17)

You might think that with all the backup Elisha had, he would be quick to dispose of the Aramean soldiers. But he handled the situation in a much more peaceful manner. What did he do? (6:18-19)

Getting Personal – *What kind of peacemaker are you? How would you have handled the above situation?*

The king of Israel's first thought was to kill the Aramean soldiers as soon as he had the chance, but Elisha talked him out of it. What did Elisha do for the enemy soldiers, and what was the result of his actions? (6:20-23)

The Aramean soldiers saw that it was useless to try to fight a people whose God could smite an entire army with blindness at will. But eventually they must have forgotten the lesson they learned, because they again laid siege to

Samaria. (Of course, the people of Israel had also seen the awesome power of God and still refused to repent.)

At this time Ben-Hadad is still king over the Aramean army. (This is the same Ben-Hadad that King Ahab should have killed in the last session, but didn't.) And this time Ben-Hadad attacked Israel during a severe famine. The city of Samaria was in sad shape. Food was so scarce that the *head* of a donkey cost two pounds of silver. (And the Jews weren't even supposed to eat donkey; it was an unclean animal.) But that's not the worst thing they were eating. Review 2 Kings 6:26-31 and describe the desperate situation of the people of Israel.

Read 2 Kings 7:1-20.
Joram, the king of Israel, blamed Elisha for the condition of his country and threatened to have him killed. But Elisha prophesied that the famine would be lifted within the next 24 hours. One of the king's officers doubted Elisha's prophecy. How did Elisha reply to him? (7:2)

Getting Personal — *How do you respond when others challenge or doubt you?*

During the Aramean siege, there were four lepers who hung around the gate to Samaria. They considered all their options, none of which were very good. They figured if they stayed where they were, they would die. If they went into the city where the famine was so bad, they would die. If they surrendered to the Arameans, they *might* die—but then again, they might not. So they decided to take their chances and go over to the enemy camp. What did they discover when they got there? (7:3-8)

The lepers returned to Samaria and reported what they had discovered. The king of Israel was a little skeptical about believing them. He assumed the Arameans had left their camp to hide in the countryside and would attack the Israelites when they came to check it out. (All the Israelites knew is that the Arameans weren't in their camp. They had no way of knowing that God had defeated the entire enemy army using only *sound effects*.)

After cautiously checking out the lepers' story, King Joram discovered that it was safe to enter the Aramean camp. To say that the Israelites were eager to get something to eat was an understatement. What happened to the officer of the king who had previously doubted Elisha's prophecy? (7:17-20)

Read 2 Kings 8:1-29.
Before the famine, Elisha had warned the woman who provided him a home to leave town. She and her family moved away for seven years, and when they returned she discovered that someone had taken possession of her house and property. As she went to see the king and get some help, she found herself involved in an example of God's perfect timing. Why was her arrival at the palace so well-timed? (8:3-6)

Sometime after the famine and the Aramean siege, Ben-Hadad became sick. Elisha was in the area, so Ben-Hadad sent a messenger with a gift, asking Elisha to inquire of God whether or not he would recover from his illness. The name of Ben-Hadad's messenger was Hazael. Elisha told Hazael that Ben-Hadad would recover from his illness, but that he would die. Then Elisha began to stare at Hazael and to cry. Why did Elisha cry? (8:10-12)

Getting Personal — *What does this passage tell you about the appropriateness of expressing tears and sad emotions?*

How did Elisha's prophecy (that Ben-Hadad was going to recover from his illness, but that he was also going to die) come true? (8:13-15)

With Joram king in Israel and Hazael king in Aram, it seems that the only decent king around was Jehoshaphat, in Judah. But then Jehoshaphat died and the kingdom went to Jehoram, his oldest son. Jehoram was by no means the kind of king his father had been. In fact, the king he is compared to is the evil Ahab (8:18). Jehoram's eight-year reign was marked by rebellion and conflict.

Read 2 Kings 9:1-10.
Jehoram was followed by his son, Ahaziah. (The Ahaziah mentioned in 1 Kings 22:51–2 Kings 1:18 was the son of Ahab and the king of Israel. This Ahaziah in 2 Kings 8:25–9:29 was the son of Jehoram and the king of Judah.) Ahaziah was another wicked king. It so happened that Israel and Judah were allies at this time. They saw the need to combine their forces to fight against Hazael, the new king of Aram. Israel's king, Joram, was wounded in the battle, so Ahaziah went to visit him. Little did either of them know that they would both soon be dead at the hands of a newly appointed king of Israel. Who was to be the next king of Israel, and what was his mission going to be? (9:1-10)

Cleaning Up the Kingdom
Read 2 Kings 9:11-37.
This new king was the first in a while who had been anointed by a prophet as God's choice for the position. Most of the kings you've seen lately have just sort of inherited the job. You may also notice that Jehu's father's name was

Jehoshaphat, but note that this isn't the same Jehoshaphat who was previously king of Judah. (Isn't it tough trying to keep up with all these names that are similar or the same?)

Jehu was a commander in the army of Israel, and he must have been popular with the other men. As soon as his fellow officers discovered that he had been anointed king, they gave him their support immediately. But Jehu wanted to keep things quiet until he could "surprise" Joram.

Joram was recuperating at his quarters in Jezreel when Jehu's troops approached the city. A lookout saw them coming and Joram sent a messenger out to see what was going on. Jehu told the messenger to fall in behind him. The lookout saw what happened and told Joram, who sent a second messenger to try to find out if this group of soldiers was coming in peace. Jehu also had the second messenger fall in behind him. By this time Jehu was close enough for the lookout to tell who it was. How did the lookout know it was Jehu? (9:20)

Joram and Ahaziah took separate chariots and went out to meet Jehu. Where did they happen to meet him? (9:21)

What happened then? (9:22-26)

(The death of Joram was the fulfillment of Elijah's prophecy against Ahab that God postponed to a later generation [1 Kings 21:29].) Ahaziah tried to get away. But before he did, Jehu gave chase and wounded him. He soon died from his wound.

And still Jehu wasn't finished. He knew he still needed to deal with Jezebel, who by this time knew he was coming and was waiting for him. In fact, she had painted up her eyes and fixed her hair. And when Jehu got within earshot, she sarcastically called Jehu by the name "Zimri." (You may remember that Zimri was the king of Israel who ruled only seven days before dissension led him to commit suicide [1 Kings 16:15-20].) But Jezebel shouldn't have been quite so sassy. What happened to her? (2 Kings 9:30-33)

In spite of her wickedness, Jehu thought her body deserved a burial—if for no other reason than she had been the daughter of a king. But what prevented a decent burial? (9:34-37)

Jehu's job was still not finished. He was supposed to destroy the entire house of Ahab and insure that no male descendants were left to inherit the kingdom. (Again, this was God's judgment on Ahab for his extreme cruelty in taking over Naboth's vineyard [1 Kings 21:17-22].) The problem was that Ahab had 70 male descendants. But Jehu was in a good position to bargain. After all, he had just killed the king of Israel as well as the king of Judah, so the city officials in Samaria (where the sons of Ahab lived) were willing to cooperate and avoid any more trouble.

Read 2 Kings 10:1-36.
Then Jehu got a little sneaky. He wrote a letter to the leaders of Samaria and told them that if they really wanted to cooperate with him, they would "take the heads of your master's [Ahab's] sons and come to me in Jezreel by this time tomorrow" (2 Kings 10:6). Jehu's message could be taken in two ways. Did he want the Samaritans to take the prominent people from among the 70 sons of Ahab to go meet with Jehu the next day? Or did he want 70 heads sent next-day delivery?

How did the officials of Samaria interpret the letter? (10:6-8)

The next day, after the Samaritans had responded to his letter, Jehu went out to talk to them. Jehu first declared the people innocent of the death of their king. He accepted blame for that action. But what did he say about the 70 heads piled up at the city gate? (10:9)

Jehu killed everyone connected with Ahab. He then found 42 relatives of Ahaziah and had them killed too. After eliminating the wickedness from the royal lines, Jehu turned his attention to wickedness in the priesthood. He got the attention of the people by saying something to the effect of: "You thought Ahab was devoted to Baal? Just wait and see how much I am going to serve him." Then what did Jehu do? (10:18-27)

In summary, Jehu was responsible for eliminating Baal worship in Israel, but he still didn't get rid of the golden calves that had been established as worship objects by King Jeroboam years before. Consequently, God began to reduce the size and power of Israel. Hazael, the Aramean king who killed and replaced Ben-Hadad, began to overpower the Israelites in several different places. And in the next session, you will see the continued deterioration of the nation of Israel. But try not to worry about that now. Let's worry about worry instead.

 JOURNEY INWARD

How susceptible are you to **worry**? To get a better handle on it, fill in the following Worry Meters. Using a scale of 0 (least) to 10 (most), determine how much you worry, and fill in the appropriate level.

Spouse   Relationships   Physical Appearance

Your Personal Future   The Future of the World
                        (Pollution, nuclear war, etc.)

Your Parents   Your Children   Other_____

Most of us probably relate to Elisha's servant in this session. We react to the things we *see* (or feel, or smell, or hear). We worry about a vast assortment of tangible things, and then in addition, we worry about a lot of intangible things as well.

But we can learn from Elisha the antidote to worry: *faith*. Elisha knew there was no problem too big for God to handle, so he refused to worry about anything. What did it matter that he was surrounded by an entire enemy army that would like nothing better than to see him dead? He knew that God was in control of the situation and that there was no need to worry.

And when you think about it, any God who can smite one army with blindness and scare off another one by making the right noises is certainly a God we can (and should) put our faith in. But it takes practice to replace worry with faith. So for now do two things:

(1) Review your Worry Meters and ask God to take control of all those areas of your life to the extent that you don't feel compelled to worry about them anymore.

134

(2) Since Step #1 will probably take some time, choose *one* of those areas to focus on this week. Spend some time in prayer every day, and keep reminding yourself that since God is in control there is no need to worry.

God doesn't like to see you worry. It's unhealthy and nonproductive, and it shows that you don't trust Him to take care of you. So the next time you are faced with a seemingly hopeless situation, ask God to step in and take care of it. He will be there. That's one thing you'll never have to worry about.

 **KEY VERSE**

"Don't be afraid. . . . Those who are with us are more than those who are with them" (2 Kings 6:16).

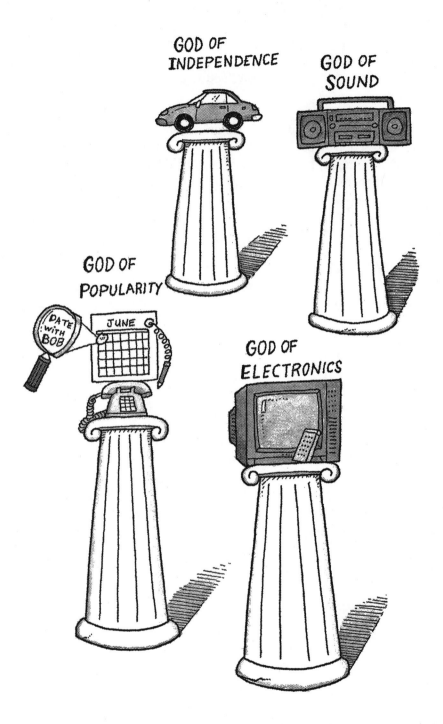

GOD OF
INDEPENDENCE

GOD OF
SOUND

GOD OF
POPULARITY

GOD OF
ELECTRONICS

*Are **you** guilty of worshiping any of these primitive gods?*

11

WHAT TO DO WITH YOUR IDOL TIME

(2 Kings 11 – 17)

Good morning, class," said the professor as he began his ancient history lecture. "Today we're going to examine a civilization that lived several thousand years ago. And we want to look specifically at their primitive forms of idol worship."

Half the class settled down for a long winter's nap, but the professor went on. "According to historians and archaeologists, the people of this time had many gods. The young women would get up early every morning and apply various kinds of paint to their faces to please the god of popularity. (This practice also pleased the males.) The males spent much of their time at a mobile, four-wheeled altar. They kept busy washing, polishing, and otherwise worshiping the god of independence at this often turbo-charged, fuel-injected altar.

"Another popular god of this era was the god of sound, to whom the young people devoted hours each day. This god had many monuments built to him—component altars at home, portable box-type altars that could be carried to the beach and other places, and even mini-altars with earphones that one could operate while jogging or going almost anywhere.

"But the most popular god by far was the electronic telegod—the god of innumerable forms and sounds. People would plan their schedules around the worship of this god, which often went on for hours at a time. Some say that this god had a hypnotic effect on its worshipers as they stared at it, transfixed."

A student interrupted: "What kind of people would be foolish enough to waste all their valuable time devoted to such stupid gods? And by the way, is all this going to be on the test?"

The prof winced a little at the student's insensitivity, but continued. "It seems silly to us now, but most of the people of this civilization were consumed by these and other gods. In all likelihood, they never put much thought behind their actions. And yes, Miss Johnson, you will be expected to know all this for next week's quiz on the late 20th century. Then we'll move on to the section on archaic forms of space travel in the 21st century."

. . . .

When we see movies about primitive tribes or look at pictures from archaeological digs and see the ugly, pudgy little idols that those people worshiped, we are often quick to laugh at their naiveté. But we're not usually as quick to examine our own lives for certain possessions or activities that may be just as idolatrous. You'll have the opportunity to think about your own idols a little later. First, let's take a look at Israel's continued problems with idolatry.

 JOURNEY ONWARD
Read 2 Kings 11:1-21.
Previous sessions have zipped through so many kings so quickly that you are probably more than a little confused by now. And these final two sessions will continue that trend. But in case you haven't noticed yet, the royalty in Judah have been getting knocked off fairly regularly. Back when Jehoram became king, not too much was said about him (2 Kings 8:16-24). But the account in 2 Chronicles tells us that he killed all his brothers to establish himself as king (2 Chronicles 21:4). Other of his family members were killed or carried off by attacking Arabs (2 Chronicles 21:16-17; 22:1). And you may remember that Jehu killed 42 members of the house of Judah (2 Kings 10:12-14).

And after Jehu killed Ahaziah, more killing came from within. Ahaziah's mother, Athaliah, saw opportunity for advancement, and she decided to kill off everyone else in the family so she could rule. But in spite of everyone's efforts to wipe out the leaders of the tribe of Judah, what promise had God previously made to David that would make it unlikely that such an event would ever occur? (2 Samuel 7:16)

And sure enough, Athaliah failed in her attempt to eliminate all her competition. She ruled for six years, but all that time there was another son of Ahaziah hiding out under the protection of caring adults. What was his name? (2 Kings 11:1-3)

Not much is said about how Judah liked being ruled by a queen instead of a king, but the young boy hiding from her seemed to have a lot of support from the people. In the seventh year of Queen Athaliah's rule, Jehoiada (the priest) decided it was time to bring the young Joash out of hiding. He called for the commanders of the army, made them take an oath of loyalty to Joash, and armed them with spears and shields. Then what happened? (11:12)

What happened to Queen Athaliah? (11:13-15)

At this time, Jehoiada also made a covenant between God and the new king, promising that the people of Judah would be God's people. And the people of Judah were in agreement. How did they show their devotion to God? (11:17-20)

Getting Personal —*How do you show your devotion to God?*

How old was King Joash at this time? (11:21)

Read 2 Kings 12:1-21.
What was the first big project King Joash undertook? (12:4-5)

At first, Joash couldn't gather enough funds to finance his project. But that didn't stop his plans. What did he do to raise more money? (12:9-12)

What kind of people were the men who were working on restoring the temple? (12:13-15)

Read 2 Chronicles 24:17-25.
But the spiritual renewal of Judah seemed to be generated primarily by the priest, Jehoiada, and not (unfortunately) by King Joash. Sometime later, Jehoiada died. What happened then? (2 Chronicles 24:17-19)

After Jehoiada's death, God addressed the people of Judah through Jehoiada's son, Zechariah. What happened to Zechariah? (24:20-22)

And after Joash's cruel treatment of Zechariah, it wasn't long before Joash faced trouble of his own. Because Judah had again forsaken God, they were faced with another battle against the army of Hazael, King of Aram. How did Joash prevent attack? (2 Kings 12:17-18)

But Joash's action only postponed the problem; it didn't eliminate it. When the Aramean army finally attacked Jerusalem, what were the results? (2 Chronicles 24:23-25)

Read 2 Kings 13:1-25.
So after a promising start as king of Judah, Joash came to a rather unspectacular end. And while Judah was suffering because of the Aramean army, so was Israel. Jehu's son, Jehoahaz, had become king. He was another rotten king to add to the already long list of evil leaders to date. But to the credit of Jehoahaz, he turned back to God when the Aramean army began to severely oppress Israel. And even though God delivered Israel from Aram, the people still refused to turn away from their false worship practices. And their army had been almost eliminated. What did they have left? (2 Kings 13:4-7)

Jehoahaz was succeeded by his son, Jehoash—another bad king to add to the list. But recorded with the short reference to Jehoash is a reference to someone whose name hasn't come up in a while—Elisha. The prophet was just about to die when Jehoash went to see him for a little military help. What did Elisha predict for Israel? (13:17)

What half-hearted response did Jehoash make to Elisha's request that limited the success Israel had against the nation of Aram? (13:18-19)

Later Elisha's prophecy came true as Israel defeated Aram three times (2 Kings 13:25). By then, Elisha had died. But even after death he was the source of an amazing miracle. Review 2 Kings 13:20-21 and record the details of the remarkable event.

Read 2 Kings 14:1-29.
Meanwhile, Judah had a new king—Amaziah, the son of Joash. And this king wasn't all bad. (He wasn't all good, either, but at this point every halfway decent king is worth noting.) While previous kings had been losing territory that rightly belonged to Judah, Amaziah was able to get some of it back (2 Kings 14:7). But after initial success as a military leader, Amaziah decided to go to battle against Jehoash, the king of Israel. Jehoash tried to talk Amaziah out of it, but Amaziah wouldn't listen. What happened? (14:8-14)

Skim 2 Kings 15:1-38.
After Amaziah's failure, he was killed as the result of a conspiracy (14:17-20). He was followed by a succession of less-than-outstanding kings of Judah. Who succeeded Amaziah, what kind of king was he, and what was unique about him? (15:1-5)

Who was the next king of Judah and what kind of guy was he? (15:32-35)

Read 2 Kings 16:1-20.
During this time, Judah began to receive more oppression by their enemies. And apparently much of the opposition was deserved because the new king of Judah was one of the worst. What was his name and what did he do that was so terrible? (16:1-4)

Read 2 Chronicles 28:22-25.
And as if the sacrificial practices of Ahaz weren't bad enough, he also made an alliance with the king of Assyria that involved giving away much of the remaining silver and gold in the temple as well as incorporating Assyrian worship practices in the temple. What other detestable practices was Ahaz guilty of? (2 Chronicles 28:22-25)

Israel's Kings
Meanwhile, the kings of Israel weren't having much better success than the kings of Judah. Read each of the following passages and list the names of the Israelite kings and any significant events from their reigns.

❏ 2 Kings 14:23-27

❏ 2 Kings 15:8-10

❏ 2 Kings 15:13-16

❏ 2 Kings 15:17-20

❏ 2 Kings 15:23-25

❏ 2 Kings 15:27-30

❏ 2 Kings 17:1-6

As you could tell from reading through these accounts of the last kings of Israel, it was a time of idol worship, assassinations, and other various evil activity. And when you think about it, God's patience seems almost unlimited. But not quite.

Getting Personal – *What kinds of evil practices are evident among the leaders of our country today? How long do you think God will be patient with those leaders?*

Read 2 Kings 17:1-41.
After being delivered out of bondage in Egypt, receiving their own Promised Land, and being granted their demand for a king, the people absolutely refused to worship the God who had made it all possible. God sent prophets to warn the people and to perform great signs (such as fire falling from heaven and the parting of the Jordan River), but the people still refused to straighten out their spiritual lives. God allowed the Israelites to experience minor defeats to indicate the importance of their actions. Still no response. And as a result, God finally allowed His people to go back into captivity.

But just in case someone is skimming through the Books of Kings and misses the repeated accounts of the evil of the time, those events are summarized in 2 Kings 17:7-17. Review this passage and make a list of the specific sins committed by the Israelites.

The Assyrian kings who took the Israelites into captivity were smart. They not only took the Israelites out of the country, they sent back some of their own people to settle there. But when the Assyrians first tried to settle in Samaria, they faced a major problem. What was the problem, and what was causing it? (17:25)

How did they take care of the problem? (17:26-28)

The Assyrians learned the hard way that the God of Israel was a powerful force to be reckoned with, but they just incorporated the worship of God into the worship practices of their other gods.

Judah had not yet been taken into captivity at this time. But according to 2 Kings 17:18-19, Judah was not keeping God's commandments either. We'll find out in the next session what happens to Judah.

 JOURNEY INWARD

This session and the next one clearly point out what can be expected from a prolonged devotion to **idols**. Time after time God had warned the Israelites to get rid of their idols and to discontinue their worship of other gods. But the people refused to listen to prophets and good kings who had tried to get them back on the right path.

In short, an extended dedication to idols leads to captivity. The one thing that was supposed to separate Israel and Judah from the surrounding nations was their belief in a powerful, living God. But after they deserted God, they lost their distinction (and their power). And without the power of God behind them, they became "easy pickings" for large nations with trained soldiers.

The same principles work today. If you claim to be a Christian, you should be distinctive from the non-Christians around you. You shouldn't have a superior attitude, but your priorities should be different. You shouldn't covet the same "idols" as the rest of the people you know, whether those idols are clothes, cars, money, or whatever.

If your image of an "idol" is an ugly stone figure that sits in a cave, you need to rethink your definition. An idol is anything that takes more of your time and attention than God does. Twentieth-century idols have chrome wheels, designer names, and pictures of presidents on them. Using the 20th-century definition, draw all of your "idols" in the space below. (And you may need to draw your friends, your family, or yourself.)

The things you draw may not all be *bad* things. But if they interfere with your relationship with God, they classify as idols. You may not need to eliminate them from your life, but you will probably need to readjust your priorities.

Spiritual erosion is a gradual thing. You can let your personal worship of God slip a little this week and think, *No big deal.* It slips a little more next week and you think, *I'll catch up later.* And by the next week, you may not think about God at all.

Spend some time at this point offering all your "idols" back to God. Make sure He is first on your list, and the other things will fall into place. You won't be disappointed. (OK. You may be disappointed at first, but not for long.) You have to try it to see that it works. Don't just sit there idle.

 KEY VERSES

"So the Lord was very angry with Israel and removed them from His presence. Only the tribe of Judah was left, and even Judah did not keep the commands of the Lord their God" (2 Kings 17:18-19).

We don't always get second chances, but when we do, we need to appreciate the opportunities.

12

THE (SECOND) CHANCE OF A LIFETIME

(2 Kings 18-25)

Ladies and gentlemen, the state football championship has come down to this final play. Down by four points, the local Central High Hamsters have to score a touchdown to beat the Melonheads of Mongo High. Here's the play . . . the snap . . . the quarterback fades into the pocket . . . he sees Bruno Schwartzbautner . . . he passes . . . Bruno is wide open . . . AND HE DROPS THE BALL. IT WAS RIGHT IN HIS HANDS AND HE JUST COULDN'T . . . (SCREAMS) BUT WAIT. THERE'S A FLAG ON THE PLAY! WE'RE GOING TO GET ANOTHER CHANCE!"

On the next play, Bruno makes a one-handed catch on the five-yard line, breaks eight tackles, and swan dives over the safety for a touchdown and the state championship. He becomes a hero for life.

. . . .

Maybe you have a similar story to tell. Your story may not be so dramatic, but any story of how a second chance changed your life is a good one. Perhaps you revealed a secret and lost a friendship, but your friend gave you a second chance and restored the relationship. Or maybe the sting of blowing a job interview was more than soothed when you were more aggressive the second round and got the job offer. We don't always get a second chance after we fail, but when we do, we need to appreciate the opportunity.

JOURNEY ONWARD

The nation of Israel never learned the importance of second chances. For most of their history, one king after another was evil. Few were willing to address the problem of the people's idolatry. And God finally determined not to give them another opportunity—at least, not for awhile. As you saw in the last session, the Israelites were carried off into captivity. God isn't going to forget them, as you will see if you continue in Books 3 and 4 of this series. But it was becoming clear that no matter how many additional opportunities God gave them to put their lives in order, the Israelites just weren't going to do it.

So, in this session, the focus is on the remaining free people of God—the people of Judah. And the session also contains a remarkable personal example of how God sometimes gives His people an unexpected second chance.

Read 2 Kings 18:1-37.
Judah had a king named Hezekiah. His name is one worth remembering. Why? (2 Kings 18:1-3, 5)

Hezekiah's reign was one filled with problems and challenges. First of all, the people of Judah were still involved with all kinds of idol worship. They had even taken an object that was once a symbol of God's power and deliverance (and His willingness to grant second chances), and were currently using it as an object of idol worship. What was the object?
(2 Kings 18:4—see also Numbers 21:4-9)

Another of Hezekiah's headaches was the Assyrian army. Hezekiah was king of Judah when the Assyrians had conquered Israel (2 Kings 18:10).

Naturally, the Assyrians saw Judah as another likely target of conquest. They attacked Judah about eight years after their defeat of Israel. How did Hezekiah deal with the first Assyrian threat? (18:13-16)

But in spite of Hezekiah's efforts, the Assyrians were still determined to go to battle against Judah. Sennacherib, the king of Assyria, sent a delegation to Jerusalem to deliver a message—in Hebrew no less. He knew the people of Judah wouldn't want to go through a long siege. What were some of the threats he used to convince them to give in to Assyria? (18:27-33)

Read 2 Kings 19:1-37.
How did Hezekiah react to the threats of the Assyrian delegation? (19:1)

Hezekiah also sent for the Prophet Isaiah to find out what God wanted him to know. What did Isaiah tell the king? (19:5-7)

Yet Sennacherib continued his threats against Judah. Hezekiah responded by praying. He was honest with God. Frankly, Hezekiah was probably a little scared. He knew how the Assyrians had defeated numerous other countries. He knew that the gods of those countries had been burned and forgotten about. But he also knew that God was much more than a god of wood or stone. And Hezekiah determined to continue to put his trust in the living God.

Getting Personal – *How do you respond to threats? Have you determined to put your trust in God?*

God again sent Isaiah to comfort Hezekiah with the assurance that God would deliver Judah from the hands of Assyria. Isaiah told King Hezekiah that Sennacherib wouldn't even shoot an arrow or build a siege ramp against Jerusalem (19:32-34). How did God prevent the Assyrians from following through with their plans to destroy Judah? (19:35-36)

A short time later, Sennacherib was worshiping his god in a temple when two of his sons killed him and a third son succeeded him as king of Assyria.

Read 2 Kings 20:1-21.
It is at this point in the Bible that we find the great example of God's willingness to give His people second chances. Hezekiah was ill and about to die. He didn't just *think* he was about to die; God had sent Isaiah to tell him *for sure* that his illness was fatal.

No doubt at some point in your life you have been asked what you would do if you knew you had only one week to live. And if you were like most people, your answers included such activities as traveling to places you've never been, spending all the money you've saved up, telling certain people what you *really* think about them, and so forth. But Hezekiah didn't do any of those things when he heard the news. What did Hezekiah do? (20:1-3)

Getting Personal — *Put yourself in Hezekiah's place. What would you have done?*

And in this instance, God heard and responded immediately. In fact, Isaiah hadn't even gotten out of the house after delivering God's bad news when God had him turn around and deliver some good news. What good news did Isaiah have for Hezekiah? (20:4-6)

It's interesting to note that even though God had said that Hezekiah wouldn't die immediately, Isaiah still took commonsense steps to aid in the healing process. The prophet had the servants prepare a poultice of figs which he applied to Hezekiah's boil, and the king got well.

Hezekiah asked Isaiah for a sign that God would do what He had promised. So Isaiah gave Hezekiah a couple of choices. What sign did Hezekiah ask for and receive? (20:9-11)

After Hezekiah's recovery, he received visitors who brought a "get well present" from the king of Babylon. While the Babylonian visitors were in Jerusalem, Hezekiah couldn't help showing off a little. (See 2 Chronicles 32:24-26 for an account of Hezekiah's problem with pride.) He showed the Babylonians everything in his palace, the storehouses, the kingdom, etc. Possibly he wanted to be on good terms with Babylon because they would make a powerful ally against the Assyrians. But God knew something about the Babylonians that Hezekiah didn't. And He used this incident to reveal (through Isaiah) a significant prophecy. What was it? (20:14-18)

(A eunuch [v. 18] is a male whose sexual organs have been removed. This was a common practice in Old Testament times for males who would attend to a queen or other female royalty.)

Before Hezekiah's death, he engineered a project that made Jerusalem much more capable of sustaining a prolonged attack. What did he do? (20:20)

Read 2 Kings 21:1-26.

When Hezekiah died, he was succeeded by his son, Manasseh. The new king began to rule at age 12 and reigned for 55 years. You might think Manasseh would have learned something from Hezekiah about trusting God, but apparently he didn't. Instead of following in his father's footsteps, Manasseh was one of the most evil kings in the history of Judah. Review 2 Kings 21:1-9 and list some of the wicked actions of King Manasseh.

Notice especially verse 9. Under the rule of Manasseh, the people of Judah were guilty of more evil than the heathen nations who had lived there before them. In other words, God's own people were more sinful than those who didn't even know God. According to Jewish tradition, Isaiah was sawn in half during Manasseh's reign. And it was during this low point in the history of Judah that God made a harsh statement. What did God say would happen to Jerusalem and Judah? (21:10-15)

After Manasseh died, his son, Amon, became king. Amon wasn't much better than his father. After two years as king, he was assassinated by his own officials. The people killed off his murderers and made his son, Josiah, the new king.

Young King Josiah
Read 2 Kings 22:1-20.

Josiah got started as king early in life. He was only eight years old when he took over as leader of Judah. But somewhere he found the wisdom to be a good king. By the time he was 26 he was already concerned about repairing the temple. He took money that had been collected and delegated the work to other capable people. But as soon as the reconstruction began, a significant discovery was made. What was the discovery? (22:8)

Book of Law

152

Getting Personal – *Do you know any 26-year-olds today who are capable of leading a kingdom? How do you think their performance would rate with that of Josiah?*

The discovery was taken to King Josiah. What was his response? (22:9-11)

tore his robes

The king immediately became aware that God must be intensely angry at the people of Judah, and he sent out the high priest to see what more he could find out from God. The priest went to a prophetess. What did she tell him? (22:15-17)

What message did God have for King Josiah? (22:18-20)

because your heart was responsive + humbled yourself before the Lord ... + because you tore your robes + wept in my presence ... buried in peace / eyes will not see disaster

Read 2 Kings 23:1-37.
As soon as Josiah realized how far his nation had strayed from God's expectations for them, he immediately tried to reverse the trend. In 2 Kings 23:1-25 is a list of the things Josiah did to return his nation to fellowship with God. What was the first thing he did? (23:1-3)

Read Book of Law to people

What was the next thing Josiah did? (23:4)

Remove idols from temple + burned them

Josiah's next action was to go throughout the land tearing down altars to other gods, grinding up idols, and putting pagan priests to death. As you read through this section, you will see that offerings were being made to gods (Baal, Asherah, Molech, Chemosh, etc.) as well as to the sun, moon, stars, and constellations. Male shrine prostitutes were practicing and women were weaving to the glory of the goddess Asherah. Previous kings of Judah had dedicated horses and chariots to the sun. An altar stood so people could offer their children in the fire to the god Molech. It seems that everywhere Josiah looked he saw idol worship and a complete lack of reverence for God.

Josiah defiled all the pagan altars by burning human bones on them. He got the bones from tombs in the area, but he stopped at one particular tombstone to ask whose it was. He was told it belonged to a man of Judah. Review 1 Kings 13:1-6, 26-32 and remember who this man of Judah was. He had predicted to King Jeroboam almost 300 years ago that a king named Josiah would come to remove a lot of the false worship practices instituted by Jeroboam. And when Josiah was reminded of the story, he made sure the prophet's grave remained undisturbed.

After Josiah had discontinued all the rituals that shouldn't have been practiced, he reinstituted one that *should* have been (but hadn't been since the days of the judges). What was it? (23:21-23)

What does the Bible say in summary of Josiah's life? (23:25)

But Josiah's intense devotion couldn't make up for all the sin that had taken place prior to his reign—especially the horrendous sins of King Manasseh. Josiah's faithfulness postponed the judgment of God on Judah, but it did not remove it. After Josiah died, Judah was ruled for about 22 years by a succession of kings—Jehoahaz (3 months), Jehoiakim (11 years), Jehoiachin (3 months), and Zedekiah (11 years). These were all evil leaders, and during their reigns Judah grew weaker as it was oppressed by Egypt and then Babylon. Jehoahaz was carried off to Egypt where he died. Jehoiachin surrendered to the Babylonians and was carried off a captive (along with all the valuables from the temple). And Zedekiah was made king of Israel by the king of Babylon, a man named Nebuchadnezzar.

Skim 2 Kings 24:1–25:30.
Review 2 Kings 25:1-26 and summarize the events during the last days of Judah.

After reading through the previous section, you're bound to be wondering why the emphasis of this session is on second chances. It seems that it's all over for Judah. Yet the Book of 2 Kings ends on a somewhat optimistic note. Even in captivity, King Jehoiachin is finding favor with the Babylonian leaders. (See 2 Kings 25:27-30.) And the parallel account in 2 Chronicles 36:21-23 moves in fast forward to a point in the future where the people of God in captivity have the opportunity to return to their homeland. So the wayward people of Israel and Judah *will* be given yet another opportunity to repent and be forgiven. But in the meantime, they are going to have to suffer at the hands of enemy nations.

 JOURNEY INWARD

You may have noticed by now that in many cases God gives us **second chances** when we mess up because He is loving and forgiving—*not* because we deserve them. Hezekiah did nothing to *deserve* another 15 years of life, yet God heard his prayer and responded.

How about *your* life? Have you ever experienced the exhilarating feeling of getting a second chance that you knew you didn't deserve? If you're a Christian, you should know the feeling. Whether or not you realize all that is involved, God has saved you from a life of guilt, despair, and hopelessness; He has made it possible to replace those negative feelings with His love and forgiveness. But sometimes we lose sight of all that God has done for us. We become like the people of Judah who had lost the Book of the Law and didn't even know it. The purpose of *this* book is to help make you more like Josiah—aware of what the Bible really says and better able to respond to it.

In this area of second chances, there are a number of ways you may need to respond. First of all, are you sure you're a Christian? If not, that's the first step you need to take to receive God's greatest second chance. If you *are* a Christian, spend some time thinking about how your life is different because of your relationship with Jesus. Jot down some of those things below.

Second, Hezekiah asked God for a specific second chance to deal with a particular crisis he was facing. In your relationship with God, are there any situations you've messed up where you'd like another chance? If so, write them below and ask God to forgive you for each one.

Third, do you need to go to someone and ask for another chance in your relationship? If so, write the person's name below along with a specific time *this week* when you will go talk to him or her.

Finally, in your relationships with others, think of the people to whom *you* need to give a second chance. Are you holding grudges or making life miserable for anyone? If so, put their names below and a time when you will go this week and straighten things out with them.

There are too many times when you won't get a second chance to correct a mistake or right a wrong. So it is essential that you take advantage of as many opportunities as you can get. And if your life has been devastated by a past mistake, the first session of Book 3, *Tunes, Tales, and Truths*, will deal with how to start over again.

 **KEY VERSE**

"So Judah went into captivity, away from her land" (2 Kings 25:21).

BEFORE YOU LEAVE

Before you toss this book on your shelf and forget about it, would you take a couple of minutes to fill out the survey on page 179? We value your input on our products as we try to target our materials for your specific needs. Please let us know what you think.

And if you thought this was an OK book, you may want to move on to Book 3 in the **BibleLog Thru the Old Testament** series: *Tunes, Tales, and Truths.* No one will blame you if you're more than a little tired of reading about all the kings of Israel and Judah by now. But the hard part is behind you. Now that you've been through the chronological account of the kings, the next two books will cover the best literature of that era, some of the prophets, and the events after the captivity of Israel and Judah. So don't give up now. You're halfway through the Old Testament series.

GETTING TOGETHER

A Leader's Guide for Small Groups

Before you jump into this leader's guide in all the excitement of preparing for Session 1, take time to read these introductory pages.

Because the basic Bible content of the study is covered inductively in 12 chapters, group members should work through each assigned chapter before attending the small group meeting. This isn't always easy for busy adults, so encourage group members with a phone call or note between some of the meetings. Help them manage their time by pointing out how they can cover a few pages in a few minutes daily, and having them identify a regular time that they can devote to the **BibleLog** study.

Notice that each session is structured to include the following:

❑ Session Topic—a brief statement of purpose for the session.
❑ Icebreaker—an activity to help group members get better acquainted with the session topic and/or each other.
❑ Discussion Questions—a list of questions to encourage group participation.
❑ Optional Activities—supplemental ideas that will enhance your study.
❑ Assignment—directions for preparation and suggestions for memorization of key Scriptures.

Here are a few tips that can lead to more effective small group studies:

❑ Pray for each group member, asking the Lord to help you create an open atmosphere, so that everyone will feel free to share with each other and you.
❑ Encourage group members to bring their Bibles to each session. This series is based on the *New International Version*, but it is good to have several translations on hand for purposes of comparison.
❑ Start on time. This is especially important for the first meeting because it

will set the pattern for the rest of the course.

❏ Begin with prayer, asking the Holy Spirit to open hearts and minds and to give understanding so that Truth will be applied.

❏ Involve everyone. As learners, we retain only 10 percent of what we hear, 20 percent of what we see, 65 percent of what we hear and see, *but* 90 percent of what we hear, see, and do.

❏ Promote a relaxed environment. Arrange your chairs in a circle or semi-circle. This promotes eye contact among members and encourages more dynamic discussion. Be relaxed in your own attitude and manner.

Session Topic: God allows us to live with the consequences of our actions.

Icebreakers *(choose one)*
1. Share a time when you made a decision that resulted in dramatic (and unexpected) consequences.
2. Identify some people or things that influence your decision-making. Observe whether positive influences usually result in positive decisions and good results.

Discussion Questions
1. Discuss Samuel's list of negatives regarding the Israelites' desire for a king.
2. Do godly parents always produce godly children? Compare Hannah's method of parenting with that of Eli and Samuel.
3. Brainstorm some ways to deal with discouragement based on Hannah's actions. Why was Hannah able to rejoice rather than hold on to bitterness?
4. What are the possible results of persistently sticking with this study of 1 Samuel through 2 Chronicles?

Prayer
Ask God to help each person become more obedient to His Word.

Optional Activities
1. Have your group take the role of a nominating committee for president of the group. Divide into several teams to determine reasons why Saul—candidate for president—should be recommended to the group by the committee.
2. Encourage your group to consider the possible consequences of the choices they made during the past week. Remind them that God is full of forgiveness, but He sometimes allows us to live with the miserable results of our poor decisions.

Assignment
1. Complete Session 2.
2. Memorize 1 Samuel 3:9.

Session Topic: God wants us to look beyond outward appearances when assessing other people's abilities and worth.

Icebreakers (*choose one*)
1. Play a recording of "Frog Kissin'" by Chet Atkins. Discuss the fairy tale about the princess who kissed a frog.
2. Clip some photos of different types of people from some popular magazines. Then have group members write one-sentence profiles of each person pictured.

Discussion Questions
1. Have you ever judged someone based on a first impression?
2. How does appearance play a huge role in helping us form assumptions about others?
3. What are some ways that we can overcome our first impressions of people?
4. Review 1 Samuel 13–15 and identify the things that led Saul to his downfall.

Prayer
Ask God to help each person overcome his or her first-impression evaluation of other people. Ask group members to silently commit themselves to developing a better relationship with someone whom they may have misjudged.

Optional Activities
1. Research David's musical ability. Try to find some photos of the instruments David played.
2. Play a recording of Keith Green's "To Obey Is Better Than Sacrifice" (*No Compromise*, Sparrow) to reemphasize the Key Verse.

Assignment
1. Complete Session 3.
2. Memorize 1 Samuel 15:22.

Session Topic: God wants us to depend on Him during times of persecution and false accusations.

Icebreaker
List examples of persecution you have endured. What are some ways that people handle persecution? Discuss common reactions.

Discussion Questions
1. What was the role of Jonathan in David's life during his years of persecution?
2. How do others affect you in times of suffering?
3. What do others do that helps us during persecution?
4. How did David make right, but opposing, decisions to stand up to Goliath and retreat from Saul?

Prayer
Ask God to help each person to look to Him for strength and knowledge to react in a godlike way when facing persecution.

Optional Activities
1. Using an Old Testament map of Judah, trace David's flights from Saul.
2. Research and report on the Festival of the New Moon. Supplement the report by pointing out that this festival included a religious ceremony and was primarily a time for the Israelites to celebrate the bountiful harvests of the land.
3. Role play some proper ways to handle persecution. Ask volunteers to role play what they believe to be godly reactions to several situations of persecution.

Assignment
1. Complete Session 4.
2. Memorize 1 Samuel 18:7.

Session Topic: When we allow God to handle our vengeance, we are free to develop patience.

Icebreaker
Share a time when you deliberately set out to get even with a person who had wronged you. What were the results?

Discussion Questions
1. Examine the two opportunities David had to kill Saul. Put yourself in David's place. Would you have had the same determination to do right?
2. What principles for confrontation can you learn from Abigail's intercession for Nabal?
3. Describe David's attempts to restore his relationship with King Saul.
4. How is David's attitude toward his enemy a model for us today?
5. Describe people or situations that create in you a need to take vengeance. Brainstorm some ways you can allow God to handle your vengeance in those situations.

Prayer
Ask God to help each person develop patience with his or her enemies.

Optional Activities
1. Research and report on the occult during the early days of the Israelites. Note that God's prophets and judges warned the Israelites repeatedly that magic and sorcery were evil and dangerous.
2. On maps, trace David's flights from Saul.

Assignment
1. Complete Session 5.
2. Memorize 1 Samuel 24:12.

Session Topic: God wants us to turn costly mistakes into learning experiences.

Icebreaker
Complete each of the following statements:
The most costly mistake I've ever made was. . . .
My mistake had a long-term effect on. . . .
If I could do it all over again, I would. . . .

Discussion Questions
1. List all the costly mistakes made by David in this session. What did David learn from his errors?
2. Identify David's accomplishments in the areas of military achievement, government organization, and the institution of music in worship.
3. Read Psalm 51 (David's expression of repentance for having Uriah killed). Based on Psalm 51, how are we to approach God when we sin?
4. What was the source of the last major mistake you made? How could you have prevented that mistake from happening?

Prayer
Ask God to help each person be more discerning in making choices.

Optional Activities
1. Research the wives of David. Assign the following verses: 1 Samuel 18:27; 25:42; 25:43; 2 Samuel 3:3; 11:27; 1 Chronicles 3:2-3. You should come up with the following wives: Michal, Abigail, Ahinoam, Maacah, Bathsheba, Haggith, Abital, and Eglah.
2. Refer group members to the Attitude Check on page 168. Have them try to identify the sources of some of their mistakes. Point out that attitudes of pride, jealousy, and selfish desire are at the source of many mistakes.

Assignment
1. Complete Session 6.
2. Memorize 2 Samuel 7:11, 16.

ATTITUDE CHECK

The following attitudes are sometimes the sources of my mistakes . . .

	AGREE	DISAGREE
Pride	_____	_____
Jealousy	_____	_____
Selfish Desire	_____	_____
Anger	_____	_____
Self-centeredness	_____	_____
Impulsiveness	_____	_____
Insincerity	_____	_____
Ambition	_____	_____
Overconfidence	_____	_____
Lust	_____	_____
Hate	_____	_____
Inferiority	_____	_____
Anxiety	_____	_____
Sarcasm	_____	_____
Cynicism	_____	_____
Apathy	_____	_____
Fear	_____	_____
Others: (insert additional attitudes)	_____	_____

6

Session Topic: When we repent from our rebellious attitudes, God forgives and restores us to fellowship with Him and others.

Icebreaker
Share a time when you were a real "rebel." What was your motivation to be rebellious, and what were the consequences of your actions?

Discussion Questions
1. Put yourself in David's place and describe how you would feel if your son plotted against you.
2. What were the ingredients of Absalom's rebellion? Summarize the results of rebellion.
3. Have you ever acted as rebellious as Absalom? Were the results of your rebellion as serious as the consequences for Absalom's rebellion? Why?

Prayer
Silently confess to God any rebellious attitude you might have.

Optional Activities
1. Examine David's list of heroes in 2 Samuel 23. Point out that the number 30 probably refers to approximately 30 men. Then look at 1 Chronicles 11. Though the spellings are different, many of the names can be equated.
2. Diagram King David's family, listing his wives and children.
3. Read aloud Psalm 3. Note that this psalm is said to have been written by David when he fled from Absalom. Choose one verse in the psalm that you most identify with, and share it with the rest of the group.

Assignment
1. Complete Session 7.
2. Memorize 2 Samuel 18:33.

7

Session Topic: Obedience to God is the key factor in evaluating success.

Icebreaker
List specific possessions, attitudes, and achievements used by the world to measure success. Discuss why these items seem to indicate success.

Discussion Questions
1. How does God evaluate success differently from the world?
2. Review the furnishings and layout of the tabernacle. Compare its furnishings with those of the temple.
3. What were the sources of Solomon's affluence? How was his prosperity more *at the expense of* the people than *for* the people?
4. How do the commands in 1 Kings 8:57-58 reflect God's definition of success?

Prayer
Silently commit yourself to becoming more obedient in at least one area of your life.

Optional Activities
Read and review Tony Campolo's *The Success Fantasy* (Victor). Share some of Dr. Campolo's observations on our success-oriented society with the group.

Assignment
1. Complete Session 8.
2. Memorize 1 Kings 8:57-58.

8

Session Topic: As we learn to trust God, He provides us with courage to overcome our fears.

Icebreakers *(choose one)*
1. Read the following quote aloud: "Courage is the mastery of fear, not the absence of fear" (Mark Twain). Ask: Is it possible to master your fears without the help of God?
2. Fill out and score the Fear Survey on page 172. Then share some of your biggest fears. Complete the following sentence: The time I was most afraid was. . . .

Discussion Questions
1. List all the acts of courage found in 1 Kings 12–19.
2. What kinds of fears did Elijah experience? How did he deal with those fears?
3. Brainstorm some Scriptures that can bring comfort in times of fear and loneliness.
4. Review the characteristics of a true prophet in Deuteronomy 18. How did Elijah exhibit those characteristics?

Prayer
Ask God to help you identify your fears and begin looking to Him for help in dealing with those fears.

Optional Activities
1. Research and report on the god named Baal. Note that Baal was the most popular and supposedly most powerful Canaanite god. Baal was usually represented as a bull, symbolizing strength and fertility.
2. On a map of the Divided Kingdom, locate the 10 tribes of Israel and the 2 tribes of Judah.

Assignment
1. Complete Session 9.
2. Memorize 1 Kings 18:21.

FEAR SURVEY

Use the scoring system below to rate the fear you associate with each object or situation. Then total the numbers for your score.

	1 No Fear	2 Very Little Fear	3 Little Fear	4 Some Fear	5 Much Fear	6 Great Fear	7 Terror
1. Suffocation	1	2	3	4	5	6	7
2. Losing a job	1	2	3	4	5	6	7
3. Looking Foolish	1	2	3	4	5	6	7
4. Making mistakes	1	2	3	4	5	6	7
5. Illness or injury	1	2	3	4	5	6	7
6. Being self-conscious	1	2	3	4	5	6	7
7. Not being successful	1	2	3	4	5	6	7
8. Snakes	1	2	3	4	5	6	7
9. Public Speaking	1	2	3	4	5	6	7
10. Death	1	2	3	4	5	6	7

SCORE:

35 or less — Captain Courageous, you don't seem to have many fears.

35 to 45 — Trusting Tina, you probably have a good idea of your fear levels.

over 45 — Fearful Fred, you may need professional help.

9

Session Topic: God expects us to live honest lifestyles.

Icebreakers *(choose one)*
1. List as many forms of dishonesty as possible. Discuss the consequences of dishonesty.
2. Ask: **How many times were you dishonest in the last 24 hours?**

Discussion Questions
1. Why are some people dishonest?
2. How do people justify their dishonest actions?
3. List the advantages as well as the disadvantages of telling the truth.
4. In what way can you make Naaman's statement in 2 Kings 5:15 your own personal response to Jesus Christ?

Prayer
Take time to confess any dishonesty and receive forgiveness. Ask God to give each person the strength and ability to live truthful lives.

Optional Activities
1. Review 1 Kings 17–2 Kings 2 and list the miraculous signs that served to authenticate Elijah as God's spokesman.
2. Review 2 Kings 5 and choose a character from the chapter to portray in a brief sketch.
3. Compare the number of Elijah's miracles with that of Elisha. Note that Elisha wanted to inherit a double portion of Elijah's spirit (2 Kings 2:9).

Assignment
1. Complete Session 10.
2. Memorize 2 Kings 5:15.

Session Topic: The antidote to worry is faith that God can handle any problems we have.

Icebreaker
Share a time when God handled a problem for you. Discuss some of the physical, psychological, and emotional results of worry. Note that extreme anxiety and worry can lead to high blood pressure, stress on the heart, depression, and serious mental illness.

Discussion Questions
1. Share how you filled in your Worry Meter. In what areas are you most susceptible to worry?
2. Review the story of the Shunammite woman in 2 Kings 8:1-6. How does this story illustrate God's care of those who trust in Him?
3. How can you assure others that a force superior to any enemy is behind every Christian?
4. In what ways can you praise God for His daily care?

Prayer
Thank God for His daily love and care for each person.

Optional Activities
1. Spend some time praising God for His daily care. Begin your praise with the responsive reading of Psalm 135 on page 175.
2. Using concordances, do a study of angels. Write a description of the appearances and nature of angels as described in Scripture.

Assignment
1. Complete Session 11.
2. Memorize 2 Kings 6:16.

PSALM 135

Leader:	Praise the Lord.
Group Members:	Praise the name of the Lord;
Leader:	Praise Him, you servants of the Lord,
Group Members:	You who minister in the house of the Lord, in the courts of the house of our God.
Leader:	Praise the Lord, for the Lord is good;
Group Members:	Sing praise to His name, for that is pleasant.
Leader:	For the Lord has chosen Jacob to be His own, Israel to be His treasured possession.
Group Members:	I know that the Lord is great, that our Lord is greater than all gods.
	The Lord does whatever pleases Him, in the heavens and on the earth, in the seas and all their depths.
Group Members:	He makes clouds rise from the ends of the earth; He sends lightning with the rain and brings out the wind from His storehouses.
	He struck down the firstborn of Egypt, the firstborn of men and animals.
Group Members:	He sent His signs and wonders into your midst, O Egypt, against Pharaoh and all his servants. He struck down many nations and killed mighty kings — Sihon king of the Amorites, Og king of Bashan and all the kings of Canaan — and He gave their land as an inheritance, an inheritance to His people Israel.
Leader:	Your name, O Lord, endures forever, Your renown, O Lord, through all generations. For the Lord will vindicate His people and have compassion on His servants.
Group Members:	The idols of the nations are silver and gold, made by the hands of men.
Leader:	They have mouths, but cannot speak, eyes, but they cannot see;
Group Members:	They have ears, but cannot hear, nor is there breath in their mouths.
Leader:	Those who make them will be like them, and so will all who trust in them.
Group Members:	O house of Israel, praise the Lord; O house of Aaron, praise the Lord; O house of Levi, praise the Lord;
Leader:	You who fear Him, praise the Lord.
Group Members:	Praise be to the Lord from Zion, to Him who dwells in Jerusalem.
All:	Praise the Lord.

Session Topic: Our attention needs to be focused on God rather than idolatrous possessions or activities.

Icebreaker

Ask group members how much time they spend in the presence of each of the following idols:

❑ god of Sound (radio, stereo, Walkman, CD player, etc.)
❑ god of Electronics (TV, computer games, etc.)
❑ god of Physique (weight lifting, aerobics, sports, etc.)
❑ god of Popularity (parties, social events, etc.)

Discussion Questions

1. How were the Israelites warned about their prolonged devotion to idols?
2. How many warnings should God give *you* regarding your preoccupation with possessions and activities?
3. What would it have been like to live in Israel during the reigns of Jehu and Jeroboam II?
4. Review 2 Kings 17:7-23 and list the reasons for Israel's captivity?
5. How do idols take time and attention away from God?

Prayer

Ask God to help each person commit himself or herself to spending time with Him on a daily basis.

Optional Activities

1. Divide into three study teams to research and report on the three powerful prophets God sent to Israel to turn the nation back to Himself: Jonah, Amos, and Hosea.
2. Have the group schedule and plan out a daily time for personal devotions and worship.

Assignment

1. Complete Session 12.
2. Memorize 2 Kings 17:18-19.

12

Session Topic: God gives us second chances because He is loving and forgiving.

Icebreaker
Ask: **Have you ever gotten a second chance that you didn't deserve? How did you feel when you received a second chance?**

Discussion Questions
1. What were some of the second chances Israel and Judah were given?
2. Compare the revivals during the reigns of Hezekiah and Josiah with revivals today.
3. What characterized the revivals led by Judah's kings?
4. What would it be like to be held captive in another country?

Prayer
Ask God to give each person a second chance to deal with a particular person or situation that was mishandled the first time around. Close by asking God to help each person be more loving and forgiving when it comes to giving second chances to others.

Optional Activities
Display a chart of Judah's major kings and prophets. Create a time line to show the periods of revival and decline in Judah.

Assignment
1. Review Sessions 1–12.
2. Memorize 2 Kings 25:21.

REVIEW

Session Topic: God wants us to remember and apply what we've learned about Him in 1 Samuel through 2 Chronicles. Choose one or two review methods, based on the size and interests of your group.

Option 1
Play "Stump the Panel." Ask several volunteers to participate on two panels. The remainder of the group should write questions about the Books of 1 Samuel through 2 Chronicles, trying to stump the panels with their questions. If one panel is unable to answer a question, the question is passed to their opponents. Keep score to make this competitive.

Option 2
Use the names and places found in each chapter to play "Wheel of Fortune" or "Probe" with your group. New group members or members who missed several sessions will be able to participate since they merely have to choose consonants to fill in the blanks on a chalkboard or poster board. Be sure to alert each team whether the words are people, places, things, or phrases.

Option 3
Review by providing group members with the opportunity to raise questions, discuss problems, or share opinions on issues that had to be omitted during the course.

Option 4
Review the key verses from each session. Provide some sort of reward or certificate for all group members who have memorized all key verses.

Option 5
Have a "Royal" party. Ask group members to come to the last session dressed as a king, queen, or prophet from 1 Samuel through 2 Chronicles.

Option 6
Ask: **How has this study affected your spiritual life? How has God worked in your life during this study? Have you developed a closer relationship with the Lord during this study?**

WRAP-UP

BibleLog Old Testament Book 2

Please take a minute to fill out and mail this form giving us your candid reaction to this material. Thanks for your help!

1. In what setting did you use this **BibleLog** study?

If you used Book 2 for personal study only, skip to question 7.

2. How many people were in your group?

3. What was the age-range of those in your group?

4. How many weeks did you spend on this study?

5. How long was your average meeting time?

6. Did you complete the studies before discussing them with a group?

7. How long did it take you to complete the study on your own?

8. Do you plan to continue the **BibleLog Series**? Why or why not?

Would you like more information on Bible study resources for small groups?

Name_____

Address_____

Church_____

City_____State_____Zip_____

PLACE
STAMP
HERE

Adult Education Editor
Victor Books
1825 College Avenue
Wheaton, Illinois 60187